FURTHER UP THE ORGANISATION

First published in 1970, UP THE ORGANISATION was an instant and revolutionary bestseller, universally acclaimed by reviewers and businessmen alike. Fresh and commonsensical, it was the first book ever to awaken managers and executives to the possibility that their time-honoured corporate policies, practices and routines might in fact be stifling their employees and strangling productivity and profit.

In FURTHER UP THE ORGANISATION Robert Townsend looks at the way companies are run *today*, fifteen years on — when his advice is more needed than ever. With the same sharp, pragmatic know-how that delighted (or infuriated) the millions of readers of UP THE ORGANISATION he looks at the things we are still doing wrong and, in the age of the computer, shows us how to humanise business and, above all, make it *fun*.

D1513246

About the Author

Born in 1920, Robert Townsend had a distinguished business career as a director of American Express and President and Chairman of Avis. He retired in 1965 from managing unmanageable situations to write his worldwide number-one bestseller UP THE ORGANISATION, also published by Coronet Books.

And God created the Organization and gave It dominion over man.

Genesis 1, 30A, Subparagraph VIII

Further Up The Organisation

Robert Townsend

CORONET BOOKS
Hodder and Stoughton

Copyright © Robert Townsend 1970 and 1984

First published in Great Britain by
Michael Joseph Ltd in 1984

Coronet edition 1985
Second impression 1985

To Donald A. Petrie

British Library C.I.P.

Townsend, Robert
    Further up the organisation.
    1. Management
    I. Title
    658   HD31

    ISBN 0–340–37757–7

Printed and bound in Great Britain for
Hodder and Stoughton Paperbacks, a
division of Hodder and Stoughton Ltd.,
Mill Road, Dunton Green, Sevenoaks,
Kent (Editorial Office: 47 Bedford
Square, London, WC1 3DP) by
Cox & Wyman Ltd., Reading

CONTENTS

INTRODUCTION TO THE NEW EDITION

Since I wrote *Up the Organization* in 1970, much has happened but nothing essential in organizational human behavior has changed. In many of the major American industries, the same kind of leaders have been rising up the golden escalators and presiding in turn over the decline of their companies, their industries, and, as a consequence, the position of the United States in the world's productivity pecking order. In their companies, the workers still check their brains at the gate.

This book is an attempt to help people change that.

Many of you have been through one or more management fads, from T-Groups to Matrix to Q-Circles. This book isn't another one of those.

It's a walk around the whole subject of how people *do* work together and how they *should* work together and *would* work together if given the chance. You can make it work in the corner of the company you manage, or in the whole company if you're the chief executive officer.

I call it participative management, or Theory Y, because I don't know any better terms, but whatever you call it—it's not a program to be inflicted on or sold to your people.

It's a way of treating everybody from top to bottom as respected adults rather than children or criminals. It asks for ideas, tries them out, and rewards the employees as a group, and from time to time singles out individuals in front of their peers and says, "Thanks!"

A lot of people bought copies of *Up the Organization* and I've heard from many who have used it successfully in small and medium-sized companies. Predictably, however, among the Fortune 1000 it fell on deaf ears.

Now I've revised and updated the book and added almost 30 new chapters.

Here, then, are the essentials for creating a well-managed company—what to do, how to do it, and why—for boards of directors, chief executive officers, presidents, vice-presidents, division and department heads, managers, and employees.

This is your last chance. I'm not going to tell you again!

MEMORANDUM

To: *The Reader*
From: *The Author*
Subject: *How to Use* Up the Organization

This book is in alphabetical order. Using the table of contents, which doubles as the index, you can locate any subject on the list in thirteen seconds. And you can read all I have to say about it in five minutes or less.

Dip into it someplace.* If you don't get at least a hollow laugh *and* a sharpened need to kick that 200-foot sponge you work for, then throw the book away. It's not for you. There are already too many organizational orthodoxies imposed on people, and I don't want to help the walking dead institute another one.

In the average company the folks in the mailroom, the president, the vice-presidents, and the steno pool have three things in common: they are docile, they are bored, and they are dull. Trapped in the pigeonholes of organization charts, they've been made slaves to the rules of private and public hierarchies that run mindlessly on and on because nobody can change them.

*On second thought, read "People" first—it's the place to start.

So we've become a nation of office boys. Monster corporations like General Motors and monster agencies like the Defense Department have grown like cancer until they take up nearly all of the living working-space. Like clergymen in Anthony Trollope's day, we're but mortals trained to serve immortal institutions.

This is not our natural state. Most of us come from good solid European stock whose record of rapacity, greed, cruelty, and treachery would make Genghis Khan look like Mahatma Gandhi. To go down now without a whimper (much less a bang) is completely out of character.

Two solutions confront each of us:

Solution One *is the cop-out: you can decide that what is must be inevitable; grab your share of the cash and fringes; and comfort yourself with the distractions you call leisure.*

Solution Two *is nonviolent guerrilla warfare: start dismantling our organizations where we're serving them, leaving only the parts where they're serving us. It will take millions of such subversives to make much difference.*

This book is about Solution Two.

It's for those who have the courage, the humor, and the

energy to make a non-monster company, or a non-monster piece of a monster company, operate as if people were human.

All you need is a talent for spotting the idiocies now built into the system. But you'll have to give up being an administrator who loves to run others and become a manager who carries water for his people so they can get on with the job. And you'll have to keep a suspicious eye on the phonies who cater to your uncertainties or feed your trembling ego on press releases, office perquisites, and optimistic financial reports. You'll have to give substance to such tired rituals as the office party. And you'll certainly have to recognize, once you get a hunk of your company's stock, that you aren't the last man or woman who might enjoy the benefits of shareholding. These elegant simplicities require a sense of justice that won't be easy to hang on to.

I wrote this book when I realized how friends in one small company were being diverted by the glitter of the monster models: *if Time Inc. puts its executives in fancy offices, that must be the way to be big*. Model-watching has both a crude and subtle influence upon people at every level in every kind of work. To help start a countermovement in that company, I Xeroxed a draft of this book and left a copy on each desk before anybody got to work.

If you master each section and focus your imagination on helping your employees get everything they can deserve, you and they will probably come back to life and get rich.

Don't blame me if that doesn't solve any of your problems.

A   ACCOUNTING AND REPORTING

Developing participative management in line with Theory Y (*see* People) in a big company calls for some creative insulation from the effects of accounting and reporting.

Take a company that closes the books every month. The big honchos get their reports three weeks later, and if Plant A is worse than budget, the chain of command descends on it with a clatter and takes over. No more "We want your ideas; we want you to solve your own problems."

A layoff can be ordered just so some V.P. can anticipate the Big Guy's expected question: "Well, what are you *doing* about it?"

If you start a participative management effort at Plant A, you also have to exempt Plant A from this kind of authoritarian intervention at the first sign of trouble.

If it were my company, I'd have a V.P. of Theory Y plants, whose job would be to protect the ones undergoing change. This would also protect Plant A from having their plant manager suddenly yanked out and replaced by some *Achtung!* type, thereby blowing a couple of years' work.

When accounting runs away with the company (and this happens a lot) the situation must be changed. The chief executive officer must put the accountants in their place by firm and direct action. Accountants can be smarter than anybody else or more ambitious or both, but essentially they are bean counters—their job is to serve the operations. They can't run the ship.

Budgets, for instance. Budgets are based on little more than the past and some guesses. Yet they are treated with reverence by accountants and by incompetent chief executive officers. This can lead to all sorts of unseemly behavior by a bunch of people who can't even get the "actuals" out on time without major errors.

And how about expense accounts? If you trust one of your colleagues, for example, with a $100 million capital program, why should you let your accountants hassle him about a $73 expense account item? Isn't that a bit like trusting the maid with your children's lives but fearing she'll steal a five-dollar bill if you leave it on the hall table?

ACQUISITIONS I:
HOW TO PICK 'EM

The best acquisitions will look overpriced and you'll be tempted to veto them on that score. Don't—not if everything else looks right.

The bag of snakes will come disguised as an ever-loving blue-eyed bargain.

ACQUISITIONS II:
LOCK UP THE LAWYERS

Memorandums of intent are devilish devices that boost legal fees and cut the chances of a deal's going through.

When two companies have reached an agreement, the two principals and their lawyers, accountants, and other necessary associates should meet and start drawing up the final contract—not a memorandum of intent to agree.

I don't know how much time and effort I wasted before discovering that deals aren't usually blown by principals; they're blown by lawyers and accountants trying to prove how valuable they are.

If nobody gets to go home for dinner or if the possibility arises of having to cancel that Saturday-morning golf game, you'll be surprised how quickly problems are solved.

If the two groups split up for the weekend, their lawyers will have dreamed up enough bright ideas by Monday morning to take them miles apart—even though the deal was actually in the bag on Friday night.

If everyone stays in the same room, each smart-ass idea will be rejected or negotiated while the contract is being written.

This concept is even more important in the present era of instant disclosure. When you walk out of a locked-door closing, you announce that a deal was done. Let your lazy lawyers talk you into a memorandum of intent and all you announce to the world is that if anybody wants to queer this agreement, he'd better get moving.

Don't forget the corporate seals, round-the-clock typists, and a notary public. You can't go home until that document is signed, witnessed, and notarized.

ACQUISITIONS III: BAD / GOOD

BAD

ITT bought Levitt, a builder of tract homes. I remember Levitt from my Long Island boyhood as a creator of beautiful $15,000 houses which didn't look alike.

A top Levitt officer told me what happened.

"We got fascinated with the huge monthly report we had to fill out.* Soon our top people were all spending more time on that than on our business. We lost the feel of land trends and prices in our areas. When our figures began to slip, ITT pressured us into using cheaper materials and labor. Finally we had to liquidate what we called 'our future': the tracts of land we had bought years before at low prices. When our business and our reputation for quality were gone, they dumped us."

ITT gave too much weight to numbers and not enough to people. Harold Geneen always made me think of Bob Cratchit, power-mad after inheriting Scrooge & Marley, gone wrong with a fleet of corporate jets.

---

*I remember those monthly reports from ITT's acquisition of Avis. They had a four-line space under the instruction: "List all the registration numbers of all the vehicles you own or lease." At that time we had a fleet of 100,000 cars.

GOOD

Newhouse Publications liberated Random House by acquiring it from RCA, another dinosaur. Si Newhouse, one of the owners, has lunch with Bob Bernstein, Chairman of the Board of Random House, every Tuesday when they're both in town. "You got any problems?" asks Si. Random House recently built an $8 million warehouse after an eleven-minute phone conversation with Newhouse. "RCA would have had three experts and a site committee on us for months," said Bernstein. "They weren't set up to believe we could put up four walls and a roof by ourselves."

ADVERTISING

Fire the whole advertising department and your old agency. Then go get the best new agency you can. And concentrate your efforts on making it fun for them to create candid, effective advertising for you. Unless you've just done this, the odds favor that you have a bunch of bright people working at cross purposes to produce—at best—mediocre ads. We started at Avis by asking a few people for a list of the hottest agencies. Then we called on the creative heads of those agencies and tried to interest them in the rent a car business. Ultimately we stumbled on the right question: "How do we get five million dollars of advertising for one million dollars?" (Our competition has five dollars for each dollar we have, and yet we have to pay the same price for cars, insurance, rent, gas, oil, and people.)

Finally, Bill Bernbach heard the question and answered: "If you want five times the impact, give us ninety days to learn enough about your business to apply our skills, and then run every ad we write where we tell you to run it. Our people work to see how effective their ideas are. But most clients put our ads through a succession of assistant V.P.'s and V.P.'s of advertising, marketing, and legal until we hardly recognize the remnants. If you promise to run them just as we write them, you'll have every art director and copywriter in my shop moonlighting on your account."

We shook hands on it.*

Ninety days later, Bill Bernbach came out to show Avis his recommended ads. He said he was sorry but the only honest things they could say were that the company was second largest and that the people were trying harder. Bernbach said his own research department had advised against the ads, that he didn't like them very much himself—but it was all they had, so he was recommending them. We didn't like them much at

---

*To keep people at Avis and at Doyle Dane Bernbach from violating Bernbach's vision of the ideal account, I wrote "The Avis Rent a Car Advertising Philosophy," had it framed, and hung it in everyone's office (at both client and agency). It reads:

Avis Rent a Car
Advertising Philosophy
1. Avis will never know as much about advertising as DDB, and DDB will never know as much about the rent a car business as Avis.
2. The purpose of the advertising is to persuade the frequent business renter (whether on a business trip, a vacation trip, or renting an extra car at home) to try Avis.
3. A serious attempt will be made to create advertising with five times the effectiveness (see #2 above) of the competition's advertising.
4. To this end, Avis will approve or disapprove, not try to improve, ads which are submitted. Any changes suggested by Avis must be grounded on a material operating defect (a wrong uniform, for example).
5. To this end, DDB will only submit for approval those ads which they as an agency recommend. They will not "see what Avis thinks of that one."
6. Media selection should be the primary responsibility of DDB. However, DDB is expected to take the initiative to get guidance from Avis in weighting of markets or special situations, particularly in those areas where cold numbers do not indicate the real picture. Media judgments are open to discussion. The conviction should prevail. Compromises should be avoided.

Avis either, but we had agreed to run whatever Bill recommended.

The rest is history. Our internal sales growth rate increased from 10 percent to 35 percent in the next couple of years.

Moral: **Don't hire a master to paint you a masterpiece and then assign a roomful of schoolboy-artists to look over his shoulder and suggest improvements.**

ADVICE TO MBA'S:
I WOULDN'T HIRE YOU,
BUT IF I WERE YOU,
HERE'S WHAT I'D DO TO
OVERCOME MY EDUCATION

1. Get some hands-on blue-collar experience. I don't think you can be a stand-out officer without ever having been a trooper. You have to know how workers think and talk. What bugs them and what gets their attention; what they need from the top and what they *don't* need.

2. Try to eliminate your own job. Nobody gets fired for saying, "They do it better without me than with me. What do I do now?"

3. Make every decision as if you owned the whole company. All your colleagues will be making their decisions in ways designed to make them look good or to give the boss what they think he wants to hear. In your case you'll be giving the boss what's in the interest of the whole company for him to hear even if he won't like hearing it. This approach will give you backbone when it's needed—and you'll begin to stand out among your peers. Don't overdo it; don't be a pain in the ass. That's not in the interest of the whole company. Be pleasant. The worse the news you bring your boss, the bigger your smile should be.

4. Please remember—you're trying to learn how to get people to use their creativity *for* the company instead of against it or outside it. If you can't get a job with the outfit you want to work for, try getting a job with the biggest company in sight. Working for U.S. Steel or RCA or Goodyear or Chase Manhattan will teach you how *not* to do it. Or try Ford Motor Company. Any organization which has seventeen layers of management and pays its workers $21 an hour to write "FOMOCO is a MOFOCO" on the rest-room walls must be worth a Ph.D. equivalency in the wrong ways to work.

5. Don't tell anyone you're an MBA. Just work harder and longer and use all of those skills in a way that makes your associates look good.

ALPHABETICAL ORDER

Make sure that whoever types your infrequent memos (*see* Memorandum, the Last) uses alphabetical order. Otherwise some of your people will go through Freudian agonies as their names rise and fall on the addressee list and they appear to rise and fall in your favor.

ASSISTANTS-TO
AND MAKE-WORKING

The only people who thoroughly enjoy being assistants-to are vampires. The assistant-to operates in a very different way from an assistant. The regular line assistant has the authority of his boss when his boss is away and can therefore make the tactical day-to-day decisions that permit the surrounding areas of the company to keep functioning.

The differences can be seen by diagramming three kinds of organizations:

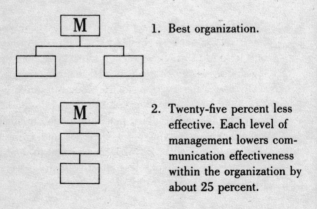

1. Best organization.

2. Twenty-five percent less effective. Each level of management lowers communication effectiveness within the organization by about 25 percent.

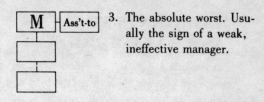

3. The absolute worst. Usually the sign of a weak, ineffective manager.

The assistant-to recommends itself to the weak or lazy manager as a crutch. It helps him where he shouldn't and can't be helped—head-to-head contact with his people. A good person deserves direct confrontation with his boss—especially when they're not in full accord. If all he gets is visits and memos from an assistant-to, he's entitled to blow his stack and go find a smarter boss somewhere.

There are some intelligent people doing assistant-to work: getting between the boss and the people who report to him, usurping power, crossing wires, and draining the organization's strength and zeal. You can't really blame the assistant-to. He wound up there because the boss got overworked and then followed his instincts. Instead of giving pieces of his job to other line officers, or carving out a whole job and giving it to someone to run with, he hired an assistant-to, and immediately became much less effective than he was when he was just overworked.

Another problem. You can't tell an assistant-to by his title. Some are called V.P. or Senior V.P. or Executive V.P. or even Chairman of the Executive Committee. But you can always tell one by the way he operates. He moves back and forth between the boss and his people with oral or written messages on real or apparent problems—overlapping and duplicating efforts and make-working.

In my book anyone who has an assistant-to should be fined a hundred dollars a day until he eliminates the position.

BIG LABOR UNIONS:
SOUNDS OF THE DYING
DINOSAUR*

A few fragments from conversations with members and ex-members of big unions:

Production worker: "In a big union shop, management is the enemy—it's something to overcome or somehow get around. That's the game everybody plays."

Machinist: "The minute you put on a blue hat [become a foreman] you're automatically a son of a bitch."

Conversation overheard in a bar: "Foreman asked me how long it would take to fix that electrode rack. Told him two weeks. Said, 'Why ask me? I'm only a mill-wright.' Sure snowed that bastard. Coulda fixed it in a coupla hours. That sure felt good."

Welder: "All I have to do is burn one rod a day and they can't fire me."

Electrician: "I remember how we used to get ready for the foreman to come in with his work assignments for the day. We had a regular plan for fucking him over by the time he walked in. As he was describing a job to

---

*If this sounds flatly anti-union, that's good. That's what it is. The big unions served a noble purpose once, and bless them for it. Now they're part of the problem and must give way if America is to move into participative management and achieve reasonable productivity. I'm sorry for the 20 percent of the working population who are stuck in the large unions and forced to work against their companies by peer pressure and "the book." Also, I don't mean to single out the industrial unions for blame. The railroad brotherhoods, the building trades, and the other craft unions are just as vicious. If I wind up in the East River wearing cement carpet slippers, however, I'd be inclined to suspect the Teamsters, one of the worst unions of all.

an electrician, you could almost see the guy chuckling as if to say, 'That'll never get wired right.' "

Conclusion: Don't hire anybody over thirty-five years old with ten or more years in a big union. It's not worth the effort to turn them around so they're working for you instead of against you.

BIG WHEELS
IN LITTLE COMPANIES

Small companies can hire big-company retirees when the man is going to exercise specific skills. It doesn't matter how big or little the company is. But it won't work with generalists. Small companies must be spartan to survive. Big companies are small companies that succeeded. Most of them have become epicurean institutions. And their fat cats have developed a lot of bad habits.

I know one small outfit that hired a big-company generalist as president when he retired. His first four acts were to:

1. *Put his son-in-law on the payroll as his assistant-to.*
2. *Order a private bathroom built next to his office.*
3. *Order a reserved parking space in front of the building.*
4. *Take his wife on a three-month trip around the world.*

It almost killed the little company.

BOSS, HOW TO RETIRE THE

The most successful retirement I ever saw was that of Walter L. Jacobs, founder of the rent a car industry and president of Hertz. For five years Walter kept telling everybody he was going to go. He turned authority and responsibility over to his younger people and built up personal banking and real estate interests in his selected retirement locale—to soak up the energy that might otherwise tempt him to be a pest. When Walter retired neither he nor anyone else went into shock. And the company made new records.

Please don't underestimate the destructive potential of the retired chief executive who remains on the premises as a "consultant" or Chairman of the Finance Committee. If you are stuck with a predecessor who has contractual rights to an office and a secretary, insist that he be physically located someplace else. You can afford to rent him a handsome suite. Otherwise neither you, nor he, nor anyone else will know who's in charge.

BREVITY

The usual way to sell an idea to a board of directors is to produce a stack of bulky reports in brown, red, black, or gray leatherette binders and hand them out to anyone who might be concerned. Days later, when the subject comes up for discussion, one third of those present won't have read the report, one third will have read enough to induce merciful blackout, and the remaining third, those opposed to the project, will have read carefully and assembled enough arguments to kill it outright or delay it indefinitely.

The next time you have to make a pitch in a board room, try it without notes, charts, handouts, or assistants. Remember:

1. *Most people with power would like to use it wisely, if someone believable would tell them how.*
2. *They know that any proposal having to do with their business can be stated clearly and completely in less than one minute.*

Why not help them out? When you know your subject cold and have a conviction, make the pitch orally. Stay under a minute. Avoid all props and end with a request for action.

BUDGETS

. . . must not be prepared on high and cast as pearls before swine. They must be prepared by the operating divisions.

Since a division must believe in the budget as its own plan for operations, management cannot juggle figures just because it likes to. Any changes must be sold to the division or the whole process is a sham.

Statements comparing budget to actual should be written not in the usual terms of higher (lower) but in plain English of better (or worse) than predicted by the budget. This eliminates the mental gear changes between income items (where parens are bad) and expense items (where parens are good). This way *all* parens become bad, and reports can be understood faster.

Most lenders, directors, and owners look at the monthly report to see if you made your budget. If you did, into the file with it. If you didn't, the report goes to an uninformed nitpicker who dreams up a lot of stupid questions. To save yourself this agony, put some arbitrary safety factor into the top statements that go outside the company. You haven't distorted the figures by which you and your managers are trying to measure trends, but you have something you can use to offset unforeseen setbacks without missing the budget as far as your investors/lenders are concerned. (*See* Accounting and Reporting.)

BUSINESS LUNCH

People seem to be afraid to meet one another except over a meal. The result is that two busy executives who need to see each other tomorrow can't get together for the next three weeks.

Solution: (1) Don't make lunch dates. (2) When you want to see someone, call and ask if you can come over now or later today or tomorrow morning. Invite people who want to see you to do likewise.

And think of all you can accomplish between twelve and two, while your friends buck traffic and violate their diets.

C

CALL YOURSELF UP

When you're off on a business trip or a vacation, pretend you're a customer. Telephone some part of your organization and ask for help. You'll run into some real horror shows. Don't blow up and ask for name, rank, and serial number—you're trying to correct, not punish. If it happens on a call to the Dubuque office, just suggest to the manager (through channels, dummy) that he make a few test calls himself.

Then try calling yourself up and see what indignities you've built into your own defenses.

CEO: PICKING THE BEST MAN FOR THE JOB

This is the most important function of the board of directors, and they must insist on using their power when the time comes for the present chief executive officer to step aside.

Usually the CEO recommends a successor and the board rubber-stamps his choice.

The new Big Guy, therefore, is picked because his predecessor and the board feel most comfortable with him.

Those are interesting qualifications but hardly crucial.

Much more important, as a measure of his future performance, is how the rest of the company perceives him. For example, is he seen as a winner who has earned a shot at the big job, or as a slick brown-noser who uses people as stepping-stones?

As an outside board member, there is no way I can discover who is the best of three candidates whom I have observed six or eight times a year during my tenure. Most of the characteristics of leadership (*see* Appendix: Rate Your Boss as a Leader) are not evident in board-room encounters.

But we must try.

If given a chance to pick one of several candidates, I'd make sure we've got the full list. ("If we had to pick a dark horse, who would we add to the list?")

I'd discourage any search outside the company (*see* Promotion, from Within). Then I'd make a choice based on these factors:

1. *Line, not staff (used to making people decisions)*
2. *Energy (he'll need a lot)*
3. *Common touch (is he comfortable listening to blue-collars? has he ever served in the trenches?)*
4. *Good listener*
5. *Strong and uncomplicated views on company values*
6. *Dissatisfied with the current state or direction of the company*

Looking back over the sixteen characteristics (including the ten in the leadership test*), it seems striking that the five characteristics which board members *actually* use to judge and endorse the new CEO have not even been mentioned:

1. *Looks (including dress)*
2. *Intelligence*
3. *Glibness*

---

*Available . . . Inclusive . . . Humorous . . . Fair . . . Decisive . . . Humble . . . Objective . . . Tough . . . Effective . . . Patient.

4. *Financial/legal expertise*
5. *Seniority*

A man can average C+ in these five and be a great leader; he can average A+ and make a wretched CEO.

CHAIRMAN OF
THE EXECUTIVE COMMITTEE

Most companies are doing it all wrong. They're wasting this title (and others like Vice-Chairman or Chairman of the Finance Committee) on retired brass. Just because no one has the guts to tell old Mr. Leatherhead (our founder) that now's the time for him to go take those hang-gliding lessons he always wanted.

These titles can be very useful.

A certain national institute was created recently. It had a young director with a good deal of experience in the field, but not much experience in managing an organization. He had his objectives clearly thought out and budgets prepared showing how and where he hoped to reach them, and what it would mean to the industry. But it was already clear that one of his problems was going to be visits and phone calls from international visiting firemen and from people in the industry wanting to talk to the boss.

He had no room in his budget for an assistant and, besides, people won't be pushed off on an assistant. He did have a substantial expense account for entertainment. So he called up an old friend who was retired and said, "I can't pay you a salary, but if you'll come in and take all these phone calls and lunches and dinners off my back, I'll make you Chairman of the Executive Committee. You can have some fun and meet some interesting people. And I can spend full time getting the institute going."

The key is the title. Nobody knows what it means. Bob Woodruff ran the Coca-Cola Company as Chairman of the Executive Committee. It can mean much or nothing. But nobody ever gets mad when the boss says, "Let me switch you to the Chairman of our Executive Committee—this is the kind of thing he takes charge of."

In a business context, I've seen this work in an area like customer complaints. People who write or call with complaints want someone to listen, sympathize, apologize, and, if indicated, correct the matter. And the higher up their complaint is handled, the quicker their fire goes out. But companies still insist on having these complaints handled by "customer-service departments" or "complaint departments" or "adjustment departments." If I'm switched to one of those, I'm twice as mad as when I called. But I'm docile as a lamb if I hear "Let me switch you to the Chairman of the Executive Committee. One of his people will take care of you. He likes to hear about all the complaints." I could be talking to the same clerk in the same department (except he is now speaking for the Chairman of the Executive Committee). And the letter of apology on that glorious letterhead not only rubs out my grievance, but retains me as a customer and gives me something to brag about to your other prospects.* The Russians have the best system. The real head of their typical embassy is a third assistant attaché, who is completely free of social obligations and can therefore devote himself fully to running the operation, while the French, British, German, and American ambassadors exhaust themselves on the cocktail- and dinner-party circuit.

---

*If you are worried about the quality of the letters, ask them to send you blind copies—but not hold up the letters for your reaction. You must be careful not to nitpick. If the letters are substandard, rewrite the worst ones and keep your drafts until you have a dozen or so. Then go in and discuss yours compared with theirs. They'll appreciate the help and their letters will improve.

CHINESE WATER DROP REPORT

Use this old Oriental torture to make things happen. If you can't get your boss to do something that's clearly in the interest of your whole outfit, and he won't return your phone calls because he knows what you're going to say, write him a note a day until he does it.

Once I had three owners who were letting a losing division sink their whole company. They got tired of my telling them to shut it down and I got tired of figuring new ways of saying it. So I made a brief daily financial report based on a dozen phoned-in bank account trial balances. The report estimated the number of days left until insolvency. They finally closed the division when the report said they had a week left.

Another time in another company, we had a chance to hire just the right man for a big problem-opportunity. He'd just retired from a competitor, and in my opinion was ready to do his number all over again for us. To make room for him, we had to take the function away from an old mossback who was sitting on the opportunity and creating the problem. Top management, as usual, was ducking the painful scene. It took ten daily notes like:

"Have you hired him yet?"

"Why haven't you hired him yet?"

"If he makes a deal with someone else for 10 percent of his time, we won't be able to use him."

"You know he's the only available guy in the country with the right skills."

"It'll probably cost us a $100 million of profit if we don't grab him."

"What do you think the stockholders would get if they sued us for not grabbing this guy? EAT THIS NOTE!"

That was the clincher. We got him and he made more than $100 million for us in the next two years.

COMPROMISE
AND KING SOLOMON

Compromise is usually bad. It should be a last resort.
If two departments or divisions have a problem they
can't solve and it comes up to you, listen to both sides
and then, unlike Solomon, pick one or the other. This
places solid accountability on the winner to make it
work.

Condition your people to avoid compromise. Teach
them to win some battles, lose others gracefully. Work
on the people who try to win them all. For the sake
of the organization, others must have a fair share of
victories.

**When you give in, give in all the way. And when
you win, try to win all the way so the responsibility to make it work rests squarely on you.**

COMPUTERS
AND THEIR PRIESTS*

First get it through your head that computers are big,
expensive, fast, dumb adding-machine–typewriters.
Then realize that most of the computer technicians that
you're likely to meet or hire are complicators, not sim-
plifiers. They're trying to make it look tough. Not easy.
They're building a mystique, a priesthood, their own
mumbo-jumbo ritual to keep you from knowing what
they—and you—are doing.

Here are some rules of thumb:

1. *At this state of the art, keep decisions on computers
   at the highest level. Make sure the climate is ruth-
   lessly hard-nosed about the practicality of every system, every program, and every report. "What are you
   going to do with that report?" "What would you do
   if you didn't have it?" Otherwise your programmers
   will be writing their doctoral papers on your machines, and your managers will be drowning in ho-
   hum reports they've been conned into asking for and
   are ashamed to admit are of no value.*
2. *Make sure your present report system is reasonably
   clean and effective before you automate. Otherwise
   your new computer will just speed up the mess.*

---

*Since this chapter was written in 1970, the computer-on-a-chip revolution has put
desk-top computers in millions of homes and offices, and made two-finger typists of
armies of housewives, executives, kids, and other folks. Notwithstanding this major
and remarkable development, the human factors remain the same and I stand by
what I said, except for the last sentence, p. 36: Because of the reduction in cost of
information-processing and communication, the risk of bankruptcy has now shifted
in some cases to those who wait too long to automate.

3. *Rather than build your own EDP staff, hire a small, independent software company to come in, plan your computer system, and then get out. Make sure they plan every detail in advance and let them know you expect them to meet every dollar and time target. Systems are like roads. Very expensive. And no good building them until you know exactly where they're going to wind up.*

4. *Before you hire a computer specialist, make it a condition that he spend some time in the factory and then sell your shoes to the customers. A month the first year, two weeks a year thereafter. This indignity* will separate those who want to use their skills to help your company from those who just want to build their know-how on your payroll.*

5. *No matter what the experts say, never, never automate a manual function without a long enough period of dual operation. When in doubt, discontinue the automation. And don't stop the manual system until the non-experts in the organization think that automation is working. I've never known a company seriously injured by automating too slowly, but there are some classic cases of companies bankrupted by computerizing prematurely.*

---

*Everybody, including the chief executive, had to go through the Avis rental-agent training school. I once saw the Ph.D. who was responsible for all Avis systems panic and run from an O'Hare rental counter at the approach of his first real customer.

COMPUTER-IN-A-BRIEFCASE: PRELIMINARY REPORT

When I wrote "Computers and Their Priests" in 1970, I was thinking about million-dollar mainframes.

Since then, of course, miniaturization (of both size and cost) has launched the Age of the Computer.

Maybe it's time for us all to get involved. For what it's worth, here's what I've done:

1. *Read* The Personal Computer Book, *by Peter Mc-Williams, New York, Ballantine/Prelude Press, 1982. The pictures alone are worth the investment. Also* Electronic Life, *by Michael Crichton, New York, Knopf, 1983.*
2. *Talked to some knowledgeable friends, who told me what I could do with a computer and made me limit myself to one application (I chose word-processing) until I got the hang of it.*
3. *Spent some time in some computer stores until I found a guy who seemed to know what he was talking about and didn't mind my calling him up to ask questions. Bought my computer from him.**
4. *Invested four Saturday mornings in computer classes.*
5. *Studied manuals. The ones which came with my*

---

*I bought an Apple IIe, Monitor III, with stand, two disk drives, Apple Dot Matrix printer with stand and box of fanfold feed paper, box of ten floppy disks, and a disk storage case. Price $3,400. My only regret—the keyboard isn't detachable.

gear aggregated 767 pages. After a month I boiled down everything I need frequently into twelve lines of instructions and pasted them on the front of the disk storage case. If I had known better, I would have opened the word-processing kit in the computer store and made them show me how to use it. If you do this, make sure you write down the twelve key instructions, because they're scattered all over the 767 pages.

6. *My wife bought an adventure game for the computer, called "The Wizard and the Princess," which keeps her up until 4 a.m.*

Keep in mind that by the time you get your computer out of the box and plugged in, it'll be out of date and overpriced. If you can't stand hearing "Oh, you've got one of those old turkeys," maybe you'd better make friends with someone who'll let you use hers.

CONFLICT
WITHIN THE ORGANIZATION

. . . a sign of a healthy organization—up to a point. A good manager doesn't try to eliminate conflict; he tries to keep it from wasting the energies of his people (*see* Compromise and King Solomon; Memorandum, the Last; Salary Review: Annual Encounter Group).

Conviction is a flame that must burn itself out—in trying an idea or fighting for a chance to try it. If bottled up inside, it will eat a person's heart away.

If you're the boss and your people fight you openly when they think you're wrong—that's healthy. If your people fight each other openly in your presence for what they believe in—that's healthy. But keep all the conflict eyeball to eyeball (*see* Memorandum, the Last).

CONSULTANTS: REAL MANAGERS DON'T NEED THEM

All a consultant says is: "I spent some time with your people; here's what they told me and here's what I suggest you do about it."

A real manager spends time with his people and *knows* what to do or how to find out. If he isn't always working with his people to improve the operation, he's not a real manager.

If you need a consultant to tell you what to do or how to find out, then *you're* the problem.

If all that's true, then why are there so many busy consultants?

Because there are so many incompetent CEOs.

I don't know why so many lawyers and accountants get to the top slot, but they do, and it's been my experience that many of them are more comfortable with their financial reports, their budgets, their assistants-to, and their plans than they are with their people.

To the extent that's true, they're incompetent as leaders.

This is when the consultant is called in to serve the CEO's important function of "management by wandering around."*

In my opinion, the number and activity of consultants are a direct measure of the trouble in our board rooms. Until we flush the toilet of top management a few more times—get the incompetents (including the lawyers and accountants) *out* and some operating people *in*—we'll be missing the fun and profit we should expect from our working lives.

In Search of Excellence: Lessons from America's Best-Run Companies, by Thomas J. Peters and Robert H. Waterman, New York, Harper & Row, 1982.

CONTACTS

A lesson very few have learned: If you want to approach the head of XYZ Corporation, call him cold. Tell him who you are and why you want to talk to him. A direct and uncomplicated relationship will follow.

The common mistake is to look for a mutual friend—or a friend's friend on his board, in his bank or investment bank or law firm—to introduce you. This starts all sorts of side vibrations and usually results in a half-assed prologue by the intermediary, who is apt to grind both edges of his own ax.

CONTROLLERS
AND ACCOUNTING

No accounting system is very good, and all of them are infinitely variable. What the controller should do is insist that management pick one system and then not let them change it. He must be very strong on this point. Otherwise the management will fall or leap into the trap of inconsistency. The easiest way to do a snow job on investors (or on yourself) is to change one factor in the accounting each month. Then you can say, "It's not comparable with last month or last year. And we can't really draw any conclusion from the figures."

In a profit squeeze, management will come up with very creative reasons for changing the accounting system. They may even call on the outside accountants for support: "Isn't this better?" "Yes, that's better." But the point is: Is it a change? If it is, don't let them make it. This rule does not apply to the *very* occasional changes *originated* by the controller to show a more honest picture.

The controller will frequently be asked for figures in a hurry. He must never lose his head—that's what managements do, not controllers. If he does prepare a hurried report, he should label it for what it is: "Prepared under pressure and not understood."

The point is that if management wants to destroy its credibility with investors and with itself by preparing quickie projections and fearless forecasts, let it do so. But any report signed by the controller should be understood and believed honest (conservative) by the controller before he releases it. The controller's job is to see that all future surprises are pleasant.

The controller should never lose sight of his function: to provide an honest notation system by which managers can take responsible action toward their chosen goals and measure their progress. Honest reports are anti-bureaucratic; they give everybody a common starting point from which to argue and make decisions.

A strategy meeting is apt to generate more heat than light unless everybody is talking from a common set of numbers.

The controller must not prepare or perpetuate reports for the Smithsonian archives. If his reports aren't useful to the line managers, they shouldn't be prepared.

From management's side, the important thing about getting the most out of the controller is to tell him about plans enough in advance so he can provide his input. Controllers are professionals. They don't gossip.

Treat them as full members of the inner council. Save lots of agony by letting the controller have a good look at new ideas before they're implemented. If controllers are elected to insidership, they'll be valuable. If they're treated like plumber's helpers, they'll get their kicks making ends instead of means out of their reports and their systems—and you can't blame them. Yes, Virginia, accountants are people.

There abideth accuracy, timeliness, understanding, and unflappability in the good controller's office—and the greatest of these is all four of them.

CONVICTION VS. EGO

Things get done in our society because of a man or a woman with conviction.

Bill Bernbach, when he was building the most exciting advertising agency of his time, had a round conference table in his office. He tried the customary rectangular one, but, as he said, "The junior men always sat at the foot and I sat at the head, and I learned that the light of conviction is often in the eyes of the junior men. With a round table, I was closer to them and less likely to miss it."

At the other extreme the economy is crowded with giant institutions—scientific, religious, educational, or artistic—that are not centers of conviction but monuments to an ego. There is probably one in your neighborhood. I have several in mind. Lots of money goes into them. Lots of good people work there. No results.

Before you commit yourself to a new effort, it's worth asking yourself a couple of questions: "Are we really trying to do something worthwhile here? Or are we just building another monument to some diseased ego?"

CORPORATE IMAGE

Among the many serious blows American business has
suffered, none was more devastating than that delivered
by the public relations man who first applied the word
"image" to a corporation and its executives. The result
has been a massive misapplication of national energy
and assets roughly rivaling the cost of a moon shot.
Grown men who should be engaged in more serious activities have been spending millions of dollars and
whole careers on silly speeches, institutional advertising, and annual reports that look like a Sunday sup-
plement.

Repent, for the Day of Judgment is never far away.
Whatever appeal may be created by a corporate-image
campaign will fade fast and sure. The only image you
should care about is the smile on the face of your customer as he enjoys your product or service, or on
the face of your employee as he gets his share of the
profits.

DECISIONS

All decisions should be made as low as possible in the organization. The Charge of the Light Brigade was ordered by an officer who wasn't there looking at the territory.

There are two kinds of decisions: those that are expensive to change and those that are not.

A decision to build the Lisa or the Macintosh* (or locate your new factory in Orlando or Yakima) shouldn't be made hastily or without plenty of input from operating people and specialists.

But the common or garden-variety decision—like when to have the cafeteria open for lunch or what brand of pencil to buy—should be made fast. No point in taking three weeks to make a decision that can be made in three seconds—and corrected inexpensively later if wrong. The whole organization may be out of business while you oscillate between baby-blue and buffalo-brown coffee cups.

*Two computers designed by Apple.

DELEGATION OF AUTHORITY I

Many give lip service, but few delegate authority *in important matters*. And that means all they delegate is dog work. A real leader does as much dog work for his people as he can: he can do it, or see a way to do without it, ten times as fast. And he delegates as many important matters as he can because that creates a climate in which people grow.

Example: An important contract with a supplier comes up for renewal. There is your present supplier and a major competitor. How many managers would delegate that decision? You're right: none. But you should. Here's one way:

1. *Find the man in your organization to whom a good contract will mean the most. (Can't be more than two levels below you—there's that bloody organization chart getting in the way.)*
2. *Take the pains to write out on one sheet of paper the optimum and the minimum that you can expect from each area of the contract.*
3. *Give your organization (including John—the man you've picked to negotiate) a couple of days to discuss your outline, edit, subtract, delete, add, and modify. Then rewrite it, call John into the office*

*(with his boss if there is one between him and you—I
assume he's in favor of this, or forget it).*

4. *With John on an extension, you phone the top man
involved at each supplier, and after the amenities,
you say: "This is John. I've asked him to negotiate
this contract. Whatever he recommends, we'll do.
There is no appeal over his head. I want a signed
contract within thirty days."*

Now, I know that ninety-nine out of a hundred managers won't take this risk. But is it a risk? John is
closer to the point of use. He will be most affected by
a bad contract. He knows how much the company gains
or loses by a concession in each area (and they know
he does). And he'll spend full time on it for the next
thirty days. Would you? I maintain the company will
get a more favorable contract every time.

Note that you've given maximum authority and accountability to John. And you've been fair to (and put great
pressure on) your suppliers by telling them the rules in
advance.

Another example: Take two kinds of executives. Fred
operates in the traditional way with his legal department. Some contracts he reads carefully and blue-pen-
cils. Others he returns with a question (implying he has
read carefully). Some he just signs. There is a feeling
among his lawyers that Fred reviews the documents

anyway, so occasionally they get sent upstairs right from the typewriter.

Bill's approach is different. He has said to his general counsel: "I don't want to read any legal documents covering transactions I've approved. If I have to sign them, then you initial them for legal aspects, and get the affected division or department head to initial for operating aspects. But remember, if you send it in with those two sets of initials, I'll sign it without reading it."

It seems to me Bill's way places the accountability where it belongs and protects the shareholders better without increasing the legal expenses. It also eliminates a lot of bulky papers that should never get in the chief executive's briefcase anyway.

DELEGATION OF AUTHORITY II: HOW TO GROW A HOT DEPARTMENT

Here's the way most companies work: I'll start the job, hand it back to you for the difficult or boring part, take it back when it's finished, walk it to the mountaintop, and modestly take the credit.

There are better ways to work.

Every leader looks for a chance to give somebody a shot at doing a whole job and getting credit for it if it works.

Why?

Because people who are normally half dead from boredom or frustration during office hours come alive when given a whole job and their abilities take a quantum jump. It's better to have champions working for you than zombies.

Example: Once upon a time I was doing investment deals for American Express. One day an important deal came in and I gave it to my assistant, Sam. I didn't sit in on his negotiations and I asked *not* to be kept informed unless he felt he needed help. He didn't. He made a better deal than I would have.

Normally, at this point I would have taken the deal to the president for approval. This time I took Sam with me and said, "This is Sam's baby. I go along with it completely, but I want him to explain it to you." He did and it was approved.

When the time came for me to report the deal to the board of directors, I called in sick and asked the president if Sam could go in my place. He didn't object. Sam went and was a success. Sixty days later, Sam and two other assistants were regularly joining me at board meetings and defending their own deals.

What did my assistants get out of it? The chance to try out their skills on important whole jobs. They also got recognition and visibility from top management. They started using 80 percent of their abilities instead of the normal 20 percent (in poorly managed companies) and they had more fun. Pretty soon they got promotions and more money.

What did I get out of it? Recognition as the leader of a hot outfit. Less time being the interface between my people and top management. More time to work on the kinds of deals that were fun for me. Pretty soon I got more money and a promotion too.

What did the company get out of it? A much more creative, productive investment department. In this case, that meant higher earnings per share.

How about the worry that Sam would get my job? Good question. I suspect that fear keeps many people from delegating. My answer is, if you're that insecure, Sam probably *should* have your job. Look at it this way. If Sam is a superstar and you don't give him a chance, you'll lose him to another division or another company. If you *do* give him a chance and he goes on to glory, he'll remember where he started and you'll have an important friend upstairs. You'll find it easier to hire good people when the word gets out that it's possible to get promoted from your shop. And even if he does get your job, chances are he'll keep going and take you with him much further than you might have gone on your own.

Important: Make sure the jobs you give your people are *whole* and *important* and that you really give them the jobs. Ask them not to report unless they're in trouble. Grit your teeth and don't ask them how it's going.

DIRECTORS, BOARD OF:
THE BACK-SEAT DRIVERS

The huge, successful company is a dinosaur, but it has one decisive advantage over the middle-size outfit that's trying to grow public; also over the established company that's in trouble enough to be ready for change. The advantage: most big companies have turned their boards of directors into non-boards. The chief executive has put his back-seat drivers to sleep.

This achievement has to be understood to be admired. In the years that I've spent on various boards I've never heard a single suggestion from a director (made *as* a director *at* a board meeting) that produced any result at all.

While ostensibly the seat of all power and responsibility, directors are usually the friends of the chief executive put there to keep him safely in office. They meet once a month, gaze at the financial window dressing (never at the operating figures by which managers run the business), listen to the chief and his team talk superficially about the state of the operation, ask a couple of dutiful questions, make token suggestions (courteously recorded and subsequently ignored), and adjourn until next month.

Over their doodles around the table, alert directors spend their time in silent worry about their personal obligations and liabilities in a business they can't know enough about to understand. The danger is that their consciences, or fears, may inspire them now and then to dabble, all in the name of responsibility.

Two simple tactics have been devised and time-tested in large organizations to head off this threat.

First, make sure that the board is composed partly of outsiders and partly of officers. Since all the important questions relate to the performance of key men and their divisions, no important questions will be asked. To do so would be a breach of etiquette, an insult to somebody at the table. Nor will any officer-director with an instinct for self-preservation (and a modicum of respect for the ignorance of the outside directors) ever bring a new or controversial idea before the board.

Second, be sure to serve cocktails and a heavy lunch before the meeting. At least one of the older directors will fall asleep (literally) at the meeting and the consequent embarrassment will make everyone eager to get the whole mess over as soon as possible. Caution: let sleeping directors lie. If one ever finds out that you rely on his somnolence, he will come to life with fierce and angry energy.

Unfortunately, smaller/newer companies often have directors who are investors or lenders able to exert the power of ownership. These directors are generally disastrous in their effect upon young managements. If not firmly under the thumb of the chief executive, they indulge a nervous impulse: they keep pulling up the flowers to see how the roots are growing.

Directors and the like (*see* Management and "Top" Management) spend very little time studying and worrying about your company. Result: they know far less than you give them credit for. What they know you can get best by a phone call. It is dangerous to take their formal advice seriously, or be too earnest about their casual questions. If they can ask important questions that the chief executive hasn't already thought of, he ought to be replaced.

Directors have one function, other than declaring dividends, which is theirs to perform: they can and must judge the chief executive officer, and throw him out when the time comes.* So the manager of a small/new company must come to these terms: he must make it clear from the outset that he accepts without question the right of the directors to assemble whenever they want and decide to replace him. Having in effect signed a resignation datable at their pleasure, he must meet with them quarterly for a whole day and report to

---

*Since this task is painful, it is rarely performed even when all the directors know it is long overdue.

them on the state and trend of the business. These four meetings and the monthly statements should enable the directors to judge him and fulfill their one significant function when the time comes.

Replacements for retiring directors should be other chief executives in completely unrelated businesses or experts active in related fields of knowledge. But suppliers of goods and services—like lawyers, accountants, bankers, and investment bankers—should be kept off the board if at all possible. Give one of these a seat, and you shut off healthy competition from his profession to serve your company.

DISOBEDIENCE
AND ITS NECESSITY

A commander in chief [manager] cannot take as an excuse for his mistakes in warfare [business] an order given by his minister [boss] or his sovereign [boss's boss], when the person giving the order is absent from the field of operations and is imperfectly aware or wholly unaware of the latest state of affairs. It follows that any commander in chief [manager] who undertakes to carry out a plan which he considers defective is at fault; he must put forward his reasons, insist on the plan being changed, and finally tender his resignation rather than be the instrument of his army's [organization's] downfall.

—NAPOLEON, Military Maxims and Thoughts

DO IT NOW

The telephone is still underused. How many times have you read something and said to yourself, "I need to talk to him"? You may never meet him, but chances are you can talk to him. Pick up the phone. Now.

You'll discover that, in this respect, the world is divided into self-important asses and authentic humans. You won't be able to get through to the former, and that's a pretty good indication they're not worth talking to. The others will be surprisingly easy to reach—and happy you called. Who isn't pleased to learn that somebody out there cares?

But call him now. While the urge is on you. Otherwise, you'll just be adding to that giant trash can of good ideas you once had but never acted on.

EJACULATION, PREMATURE

If you discovered how to eliminate air pollution for $1.50 per state, the worst way to accomplish it would be to announce your discovery. You'd be amazed at how many people would oppose your scheme. The best way, if you could stay alive and out of jail, would be just to start eliminating it, state by state.

To get something done involving several departments, divisions, or organizations, keep quiet about it. Get the available facts, marshal your allies, think through the opponent's defenses, and then go.

A premature announcement of what you're *going* to do unsettles potential supporters, gives opponents time to construct real and imaginary defenses, and tends to ensure failure.

It's a poor bureaucrat who can't stall a good idea until even its sponsor is relieved to see it dead and officially buried.

EMPLOYMENT CONTRACTS AND WHY NOT

To the company they say, "We've got him locked in, so we don't have to worry about him or listen to him as much as if we didn't."

To the individual they say, "Here's a date when your loyalty expires. Start thinking well in advance on what terms you'll renew."

Without employment contracts, the company must keep the climate challenging and invigorating and the rewards commensurate with the performance. Contracts in my opinion usually lose the men they are designed to hold. And keep those who have no other basis for staying.

ENCOURAGE TREASON

Whenever anyone says he's been offered a job by another company, don't get possessive. Encourage him to review seriously what he isn't getting out of his present job (and what he is) and see if he can better himself enough to warrant a change.

If he decides to stay, he'll buckle down and work more effectively than ever. The result is worth the week or so of inattention. And your objectivity and friendliness will help him come to a better decision sooner.

You can wince, but if you're genuinely interested in your people, how can you do anything but rejoice if they get an offer you can't match?

ENGINEERS: THEY CAN BE PART OF THE PROBLEM TOO

Big companies have layers of engineers. In designing a plant, each one adds his own cover-your-ass factor, and if you don't prevent this, you wind up with a monument instead of an efficient unit.

Another problem is that engineers don't look at design from the standpoint of the production worker or plant manager.

If you want your new product produced efficiently, better let some production foreman or foremen look at the blueprints in time to make changes.

If you want an efficient plant, make sure the leader of the team that will design and build it is the guy who will ultimately be responsible for its ongoing operation. This way, you'll tend to get a good plant at a reasonable cost with state-of-the-art materials flow.

Engineers design equipment and products, not working systems.

Remember the first law of erection: In any major construction project, the number of participating civil engineers per cubic yard of concrete is a constant.

EPAULETS FOR
THE CHIEF EXECUTIVE

With any encouragement, some people in your company will spend full time getting the chief executive decorated by foreign governments. Or putting his picture in the papers, getting him made man-of-the-year by the American Pizza Association, or press-released by some adventure in egomania like the American Academy of Achievement. A good chief executive will knock off all the nonsense. A weak one will accept the kudos because his indifferent performance as chief executive creates in him a real need for ego massage. Watch for the signs. Then you'll know what kind of chief executive you have—or are.

EXCELLENCE—OR, WHAT THE HELL ARE YOU DOING HERE?

If you don't do it excellently, don't do it at all. Because if it's not excellent it won't be profitable or fun, and if you're not in business for fun or profit, what the hell are you doing here?

EXCUSES

When you get right down to it, one of the most important tasks of a manager is to eliminate his people's excuses for failure. But if you're a paper manager, hiding in your office, they may not tell you about the problems only you can solve. So get out and ask them if there's anything you can do to help. Pretty soon they're standing right out there in the open with nobody but themselves to blame. Then they get to work, then they taste success, and then they have the strength of ten.

EXPENSE ACCOUNTS: THEORY X DISEASE

Like everything else you do—keep your expense account honest. Even if others are cheating openly. Not because you might get caught, but because honesty has to start somewhere. The people who are buying clothes or having their shirts laundered on their expense accounts are getting their fun that way because they're in a Theory X (*see* People) environment and can't get healthy kicks during office hours.

The typical response of a Theory X company to this game is to hire more people to write regulations and check the resulting paperwork. This costs more than the cheating, which, of course, doesn't stop—it just gets more inventive.

The real solution: repeal the regulations, fire the checkers, and start to build a Theory Y company (*see* People).

FADS IN MANAGEMENT: WHY DO THEY FLOP?

Management by objectives, job enrichment, team building, matrix management, quality circles—a flash of enthusiasm and then back to the old ways. Why?

1. *Top management either never understood or never got behind the effort enough to change the old Theory X culture (see People).*

2. *The experiments weren't insulated from the hostile culture around them—particularly industrial relations, accounting, personnel, and traditional company practices and policies.*

3. *The first time a recession hit, top management pulled all the controls up the pyramid and bang went your "trust me" message.*

At Texas Instruments, I was having lunch in the cafeteria one day with two production supervisors.

"If you could say 'Nano-nano' and some practice around here would disappear and nobody would know you did it, what would it be?" I asked.

"Well," said one, "I got a hundred and forty people reporting to me, but if I need a forty-dollar set of tools I gotta go up four levels and get four signatures."

The other supervisor's eyes lit up. "Me too," he said. "I gotta get five signatures just to switch two foremen who want to exchange shifts."

In the course of a debriefing with the CEO, I mentioned this (without names).

"Omigod," he said. "Years ago we had a slump in our semiconductor business and I pulled all the controls upstairs. I forgot to let go again."

FAIRNESS, JUSTICE, AND OTHER ODDITIES

Fairness, justice, or whatever you call it—it's essential and most companies don't have it. Everybody must be judged on his performance, not on his looks or his manners or his personality or who he knows or is related to.

Performances are distributed along the normal bell-shaped curve: a few outstanding ones at one end, the vast majority of satisfactory ones in the middle, and a few undeniably lousies at the other end.

Rewarding outstanding performance is important. Much more neglected is the equally important need to make sure that the underachievers *don't* get rewarded. This is more painful, so it doesn't get done very often.

You never know who is reacting to what part of your effort to be fair. Some may flee the stick and some are drawn to the carrot. It's your job to create a system that's fair.* And that's not easy. Injustice is built into our society and even into our instincts. As someone once said, the world seems to be divided into those who produce the results and those who get the credit.

*For some thoughts on keeping the president's salary fair, *see* President's Salary (Is He Really Worth $750,000?).

FAMILY BAGGAGE

The worst company wives and husbands (from the standpoint of the effect on their husbands and wives) in my experience are the overly ambitious ones. They seem to be constantly after their spouses to make more money. They don't understand that money, like prestige, if sought directly, is almost never gained. It must come as a by-product of some worthwhile objective or result which is sought and achieved for its own sake.

FEEDBACK:
TELL THEM EVERYTHING

Once a month each offgoing shift stays for an hour and the oncoming shift comes in an hour and a half early. The group of thirty to thirty-five meets with the general foremen and the superintendent. Everybody gets time and a half, of course.

Operating and financial figures are highlighted; plans and projects are discussed. Bad news is reported. Questions are answered directly and honestly.

Keeping these meetings small may be wearing on each superintendent who has to have sixteen meetings a month over a two-day period to cover the whole plant, but something like this fulfills an important part of your pledge to run a community of concerned adults instead of the usual ship of fools.

Try skipping a meeting if you want to find out how important it is. You'll get feedback. (*See* Scanlon Plan.)

FIRING PEOPLE

Firing people is unpleasant but it really has to be done occasionally. It's a neglected art in most organizations. If a guy isn't producing after a year (two at most), admit that you were wrong about him. Keeping him is unfair to other people who must make up for his failure and untangle his mess. And it's unfair to him. He might do well in another company or industry.

When someone has to go, the important thing is to fire or retire him and get him out of the office right now so the organization can start growing new muscles.

Managers often duck this duty because it's unpleasant. But purging the bad performers is as good a tonic for the organization as giving sizable rewards to the star performers. Under profit sharing, you penalize the able by holding on to the inept.

Keep in mind that first impressions of performance are often wrong. There are slow starters who become stars, and flashes in the pan who sputter out.

Don't be needlessly cruel in firing someone. Figure out a reason that is true but enables him to preserve his ego. It is usually true that his combination of skills is not what's needed, or that the job is being restructured.

If you don't feel compelled to destroy his self-regard, he can move on quickly without scars.

A good way to tell a line man from a staff man is to find out how many people he has personally fired.* If only one or two, he may be a staff man by nature. If put in a line position he may agonize for days over getting rid of some bad performer. He may hang on to one who clearly can't make it, or rig a transfer that puts a wounded, blood-hungry tiger into another part of the company. A good line man backs his gut feeling that Charlie is wrong for the job, fires him, and suffers a sleepless night or two. But the whole organization gets reinforced if he's right.

If you've inherited (or built) an office that needs a real housecleaning, the only sure cure is to move the whole thing out of town, leaving the dead wood behind. One of my friends has done it four times with different companies. The results are always the same:

1. *The good ones are confident of their futures and go with you.*
2. *The people with dubious futures don't have to face the fact that they've been fired. "The company left town," they say. They get job offers quickly, usually from your competitors who think they're conducting a raid.*

---

*Line people run the profit centers; staff people run the service departments like accounting (*see* Accounting and Reporting). It's hard to tell from a résumé or even an interview which kind of work a person is suited for.

3. *The new people at Destiny City are better than the ones you left behind and they're infused with enthusiasm because they've been exposed only to your best people.*

GEOGRAPHY, RESPECT FOR

If your business is in Cleveland, start or acquire an operation in Santa Barbara at your peril. Absentee management is fatal.

And the disaster potential is equal to the square of the distance—measured in hours—between your home base and the new plant. No matter how determined you are to visit it frequently, you'll discover that your capacity to find last-minute reasons not to go is unlimited.

If the new operation is in Europe or the Far East, the problems increase by cube functions. It is twenty-seven times harder to cope with an operation in Hong Kong than one in Duluth.

GETTING BETTER
BY GETTING SMALLER

True story. Once upon a time there was a small publisher putting out a daily newsletter. It was a typical pyramid—a president, below him a managing editor, a secretary for the two of them, and below that six editors. To get to the post office in time, their work had to be errorless and at the printer's by 7 p.m. It wasn't.

Here's what was going on: The editors would finish and take their stuff to the managing editor, who would make a few changes (otherwise what was he there for?). He'd send it to the president, who would make a few changes (otherwise what was *he* there for?). The troops had learned that whatever they did they'd have to do over, so they were giving it a lick and a promise. Upshot: work finished at 11 p.m. full of errors.

The usual solution is to add more bodies and wonder why it gets worse.

This time the president, the managing editor, and the secretary were fired. The editors were called together (by the owner) and shown the budget, including the three vacancies. "Consider yourselves a partnership," they were told. "Hire whomever you need, pay yourselves whatever the budget will stand, decide who does what—and see if you can get the stuff to the printer's without errors by 7 p.m."

For a while, work suffered because of the many meetings, but one day it all began to come together. It turned out the partners didn't need anybody else, so they were able to raise salaries an average of 63 percent (everybody in the new partnership got the same pay). They split up the housekeeping chores, named one partner to pick up everything that fell through the cracks, and discovered to their amazement that they could come in at 10 a.m. and still get the work to the printer's by 4 or 5 p.m.*

---

*"Ellis Briggs, when he was ambassador to Czechoslovakia shortly after the communist coup d'état in 1948 . . . had been pestering Washington, without success, to cut his staff of eighty personnel . . . by half. . . . One day the Czech government, unaware of this background, declared sixty-six of the American embassy's personnel persona non grata and gave them forty-eight hours to leave the country . . . to Briggs it was a blessing in disguise. 'The American embassy in Prague then consisted of thirteen people,' Briggs remarked. 'It was probably the most efficient embassy I ever headed.' " From *The Foreign Affairs Fudge Factory*, by John Franklin Campbell, New York, Basic Books, 1971.

GIFTS FROM SUPPLIERS

Right after Thanksgiving, put out the following memo in your own language and style:

There is nothing wrong with having personal friendships with representatives of those companies with whom we do business. However, this cannot be permitted to extend to the giving or receiving of gifts.

It is therefore against our policy for any employee to accept from any company or representative of a supplier company with whom we do or may do business any gifts of value, including cash, merchandise, gift certificates, weekend or vacation trips. This means, of course, returning any such gifts which may be delivered to your home or office.

Please see that the people within your area of responsibility are aware of this policy immediately.

Maybe people can keep two bottles of whiskey or the equivalent. Anything more than that should be returned with thanks for the thought.

You can avoid embarrassing your friend the supplier by letting him read the memo. Swapping gifts is an insult to him and to you. It implies (1) that he's got to con you because he's cheating your company, and (2) that you're ready to accept the favor because you could make a better deal if you tried.

GOING A LITTLE BIT PUBLIC

Small privately owned businesses are tempted in hot stock markets to register with the SEC and sell a little stock.

Result One: The stock is quoted.

Result Two: The few employees and friends who own registered stock sell or buy a few shares a week and the stock moves!

Result Three: The company doesn't sell the $15 million convertible issue that is needed for solid expansion (*"Gee, the stock is selling at $14 a share—the company is worth $60 million—why should we give away 40 percent of it for $15 million?"*). Or management is afraid to shut down the perennial loss division (*"It might hurt the price of the stock."*).

The valuation based on the tiny amount of stock traded is purely fictitious. But the mistakes made because of this purely paper value are costly. Sometimes deadly.

When André Meyer, senior partner of Lazard Frères, and I were talking about whether or not I'd run Avis for him, one of my requests (to which he readily agreed) was that neither of us would mention the price of the stock for two years. Most investment bankers, whose idea of a long-term investment is thirty-six hours, would never have agreed.

GROWTH

Growth is a by-product of the pursuit of excellence and not itself a worthy goal.

CEOs pursue growth to ensure their tenure and to increase their own take-home pay. The boss of a $5 billion company gets a bigger salary and bonus and more perks than the boss of a $100 million outfit. But growth in sales doesn't necessarily mean growth in profits per share or growth in common stock prices.*

So what's in it for the stockholders, or the customers or the rest of the employees? They wind up stuck in some wretched conglomerate which delivers shoddy goods and broken promises just so the CEO can fool the board of directors into thinking they are managing a potential growth company.

Please pursue excellence—not growth. If it leads to flat spots in your sales and profits curves, so be it. Who says human beings or human organizations don't need breathing spells?

If everyone in your company and all your customers know that your goal is excellence, then you've done your job. Keep on doing it and take what comes. Let

---

*The final insanity; In 1982, William Agee, CEO of Bendix Corporation, tried to grow by buying Martin-Marietta—which retaliated by trying to buy Bendix. Each of the companies exhausted its financial resources borrowing to buy stock in the other. Allied Corporation stepped in, bought both, and fired Agee, who had just provided himself with a $4 million golden parachute! Do you think any of that was done with the customers or the employees in mind?

everybody enjoy being part of the best even if it's not the biggest.

Château Haut-Brion didn't get where it is trying to become Coca-Cola.

HARVARD BUSINESS SCHOOL*

Don't hire Harvard Business School graduates. This worthy enterprise confesses that it trains its students for only three posts—executive vice-president, president, and board chairman. The faculty does not blush when HBS is called the West Point of capitalism.

By design, the "B-School" trains a senior officer class, the non-playing Captains of Industry. People who, upon graduation, are given a whirlwind tour of their chosen company and then an office and a secretary and some work to do while they wait for one of the top three slots to open up.

This elite, in my opinion, is missing some pretty fundamental requirements for success: humility; respect for people on the firing line; deep understanding of the nature of the business and the kind of people who can enjoy themselves making it prosper; respect from way down the line; a demonstrated record of guts, industry, loyalty, judgment, fairness, and honesty under pressure.

*Ren McPherson, a great CEO at Dana Corporation, did a stint as dean of Stanford's Graduate School of Business. He used to tell the M.B.A. candidates they reminded him of piranhas. Me too.

I've already applied (no acknowledgment) for the job of guide to the Harvard Business School in 1995. By that time, tourists will be wandering around it like Stonehenge, saying, "I wonder what they used to do here."

HEADHUNTERS

Occasionally (rarely, I hope) you may have to disregard the rule of 50 percent (*see* Promotion, from Within) and go outside to fill an opening.

If you use a headhunter, go to the trouble of writing out your description of just the person you need (in your own words, not job-description boiler plate). When he sends people in for an interview, spend some time with them, even if at first glance they're not what you're looking for. Then call up your headhunter and tell him in some detail where he's on target and where he's off. Do this after each candidate. Pretty soon he'll zero in and start sending you the kind of people you want to choose from.

HIRING:
CHOOSING FROM
THE SHORT LIST

By the time you narrow down to three candidates for the job, you're past your own deadline, your boss wants a decision now, and one of the three says he's got to tell another company yes or no tomorrow.

Take your time.

Tell the one who's pressing you to cool it or take the other offer. Get to know all of them as well as you can. Make room for it. One at a time, take them home; listen to their life stories. If your wife is as good at spotting phonies as mine is, she'll save you from a big mistake.

If you pick a lemon, it's a three-year catastrophe you'll suffer with. Of course, you tell your boss if the new person doesn't make it in eighteen months, you'll get rid of him or her and get somebody else, but it doesn't work that way. When you hire, you're filling an empty box on a chart; when you fire, it's Susan or Bill. It's easy to give him or her another year. Or so.

I was weak at selection. They all looked good to me. So I needed a strong idea to help me. It was: *Hire the one you would rather work for*. Ask yourself what you think his score would be on the boss-rating leadership test (*see* Appendix). If you can't guess how he would score, spend more time with him until you can.

Even better, find someone in your outfit who deserves a crack at the job and give it to her. It'll save you a lot of grief (*see* Promotion, from Within).

HUBRIS, THE SIN OF

Managers tend to make their biggest mistakes in things
they've previously done best. In business, as elsewhere, hubris is the unforgivable sin of acting cocky
when things are going well. As the Greeks tiresomely
told us, Hubris is followed inexorably by Nemesis.

INCENTIVE COMPENSATION AND PROFIT SHARING

Some of this may not be applicable to your business, but the philosophy is.

To be effective, an incentive compensation system of profit sharing should include the following characteristics:

1. *It should be related as directly as possible to performance. Therefore, wherever a participant has primary responsibility for a profit center, his incentive compensation is directly related on a percentage basis to the profits of that center. Where his relationship is more remote, or where his judgments are of a staff type, evaluation is based on the judgment of his boss, but this is far less desirable.*
¶ *Spend company time and effort on the preparation of profit-and-loss statements for profit centers to enable as many people as practicable to be measured that way.*
¶ *Recognize that to have maximum effectiveness, profit-center-related bonuses must be computed in accordance with an accounting system which everyone*

understands and recognizes as fair. Therefore, all overheads should be brought down to the bottom line for bonus purposes on principles agreed to in advance. In order to avoid hours of hair-splitting, review the fairness every six months.

¶ *It is most desirable that you be able to measure yourself as you go forward through the year, since you spend more time with yourself than your boss does. Therefore your percentage of profits must be agreed to in advance.*

¶ *For maximum effectiveness, no ceiling should be put on a profit-measured bonus merely because it has become substantial. On the other side of the same idea, don't let any paternalistic feeling ameliorate the situation of a manager whose business has turned bad and who, for the first time, may receive no bonus at all.*

2. *Employees who do not have sufficient funds to support their reasonable family needs are distracted from their efforts. Accordingly, attempt to have salary measure the job itself and provide enough money for reasonable living costs. Incentive compensation is to measure variations in performance.*

¶ *Within these principles, limit executive base salaries, particularly at the top. For companies up to $100 million in sales or $10 million in pre-tax net, the chief executive officer and his three or four key executives could all be within a $50,000–$100,000* top range with very little differential among them. It isn't necessary for the chief executive officer to be paid more than the other officers, any more than a professional football coach has to be paid more than the star players. It is, of course, necessary to have a chief executive officer.

3. Get your board of directors to establish in perpetuity (a moral binder) that 15 percent of total pre-tax profit will be available for those eligible* for incentive compensation. The perpetuity is important. Otherwise the finks will try to reduce it when it becomes sizable.

4. Bonuses measured by profit centers are handled by formula. Changes in formula should be resisted.

¶ The determination of discretionary bonuses is critical and much more difficult. Fairness and full disclosure are the two keys to making the system work. With this in mind:

(a) The performance of every employee with one year of service who is a candidate for bonus participation must be rated by his boss in one of three categories. It is extremely important to resist pressures to increase the number of categories because complication tends to defeat the effort to be fair. Any manager should be able to place each of his people easily in one of three categories, but it becomes much more difficult with five or six categories.

(b) Generally speaking, ratings fall in the classifica-

---

*Anyone who makes $25,000 or has other people reporting to him or her could be eligible. In a very small organization (200 people or so), everybody should be eligible.

*tion of unsatisfactory, satisfactory, and outstanding.
It is anticipated that* approximately *10 percent will
be at each extreme. Any manager whose records show
that he has no "unsatisfactory employees" may have
an explanation to give to his boss. Similarly, one
who has no "outstanding" employees over a lengthy
period of time also has an explanation to give.
(c) Once the ratings have been made, the determination of bonuses is a purely mechanical job. Each unsatisfactory employee is given a rate of zero and will
receive no bonus check. Each satisfactory employee
will receive X percent of his base salary. Each outstanding employee will receive 2X percent. Extraordi-
nary cases of multiple X percent are also added in.**
*The bonus pool produced by the 15 percent of profits
is then divided by total weighted salaries to produce
the necessary computation of X percent. An example
of how this system works: Assume a company with
3,000 employees, $100 million in sales, $10 million
in pre-tax, pre-incentive-compensation earnings. Fifteen percent of $10 million gives us a pool of $1.5
million available for incentive compensation. Assume
400 people are on incentives related to profit centers
and their formula bonuses add up to $1 million.
This leaves $500,000 for discretionary incentive com-
pensation payments. Assume 50 people are eligible
(base salary of at least $25,000 or have other people
reporting to them). Assume 4 are rated unsatisfactory*

---

*When you get all through with the 0, X, and 2X ratings, you ask, "Is there anyone
with a 2X rating whose performance belongs in a class by itself?" If there is a 3X or
4X performance, it is generally acknowledged by acclamation.

(no bonus); 42 are rated satisfactory (X percent of base salary), and 4 are rated outstanding (2X percent of base pay). In this year assume no ratings higher than 2X. Assume an average "eligible" salary of $25,000.

DISCRETIONARY INCENTIVE COMPENSATION

Eligible Employees	Performance Rating		Aggregate Base Salary	Incentive Compensation	Percent of Base Salary
4	Unsatisfactory	(0%)			
42	Satisfactory	(X%)	$1,050,000	$420,000	40
4	Outstanding	(2X%)	$100,000	80,000	80
				$500,000	

X, in this case, turns out to be 40 percent.

There were 42 people with satisfactory ratings. Each will receive incentive compensation of 40 percent of base salary. Four people were rated outstanding. Each will receive 80 percent of base salary as incentive compensation. This is an important barrier to break through. It lets some people really taste blood. ¶ This system can be prostituted and become a means of overpaying fat cats at the top. The chief executive at Avis never received a higher rating than X percent (satisfactory), and in one year received an unsatisfactory rating.*

(d) The message is as important as the money. Ac-

---

*I rated myself and then submitted the rating to the board of directors for approval. It was understood that they could lower but not raise the rating (see President's Salary [Is He Really Worth $750,000?]).

> *cordingly, bonus checks are* NEVER DISTRIBUTED *by the chief executive officer, except to those reporting directly to him. Each bonus check is physically handed to an employee by his boss and is accompanied by a conversation (preferably a dialogue, not a monologue) about the amount of the check (or absence of check) and the reasons for the evaluation. The most important conversations are with the employees who get no bonus checks because at that time one gets their undivided attention.*

Certain philosophical and psychological conditions follow from a system of the kind described above.

1. *In an ordinary economic sense, all management people are "partners" and, as such, have a major stake in one another's achievements.*
2. *There is a tough-minded attitude toward "carrying old Joe or his nephew" since everyone in the bonus system is paying for a share of old Joe or his nephew. People tend to be fairly outspoken where their pocketbooks are concerned.*

At the risk of repetition and to avoid misunderstandings, one might state the things which are *not* built into this compensation philosophy:

1. *No "thirteenth month" type of bonus or profit sharing by which every employee simply gets an extra pay pe-*

riod during the year, unrelated to performance. Such
an arrangement is worse than no incentive compensation system because it misleads the directors and
shareholders into believing that there is an incentive
compensation system when in fact there is none.

2. No incentive compensation is paid to an employee
who does not otherwise merit it because "he is count-
ing on it." Such a payment is always injurious to the
organization and other employees, since it tends to
reinforce the meritless one in the practices which jus-
tified an unsatisfactory rating.

3. No penalizing an employee—who has conducted
himself well and shown tangible results—because of
the failure of others either above him or elsewhere in
the organization. Even during loss years when the
company as a whole doesn't earn money, a few outstanding managers will receive incentive compensation or profit sharing based upon the results of the
area under their control.

4. No reducing the percentage participation of a manager because his bonus is "getting too high," since
such fudging corrupts the entire system. Your stockholders should yearn to have all your incentive compensation participants get four times their base pay
in bonus.

5. There are no secrets. No private payroll, for example.
Since at least 15 percent of your employees should
share in incentive compensation, it is very difficult to

keep them in the dark about any expenditure with which they are unfairly burdened. Because all profit centers carry full overhead, unnecessary overhead items are known throughout the organization and vocally resented. Accordingly, your executive people should have none of the following items which would reduce bonuses and cause resentment:

a) Directors' fees.

b) Executive Committee members' fees.

c) Company-paid luncheon, golf, country, or yacht clubs.

d) Executive aircraft.

e) Executive dining rooms or executive washroom.

f) Chauffeur-driven vehicles.

g) First-class air travel.

h) Company-paid travel expenses for family members.

i) Corporate philanthropy.

Your people should be encouraged to earn as much bonus as they can and then spend it on clubs, limousines, other corporate luxuries, or save it, or give it to charity. However, the choice should be theirs. Don't ask your people to subsidize the fat cats at the top.

A final thought: Please keep it simple so non-financial people who aren't in the plan but hope to be someday can understand the rules for eligibility and how the bonuses are calculated. If the bonus pool is based on divisional pre-tax, pre-interest earnings, there should be a line in the annual report income statement showing that amount so everybody can look at it.

Keeping it simple means fighting the experts. If everyone devised simple understandable systems with lots of wallop, who would need experts? When they're called in, they invariably opt for more complexity. Then people don't understand it. Then they assume they are being screwed. Then they are not motivated.

Same problem with changing the rules or the percentages. Every change means suspicion, loss of understanding, loss of trust, loss of motivation.

We all understand, of course, that the experts will agree with everything I've said and then come back with a complicated plan that changes every year.

INDIRECTION:
DON'T NEGLECT IT

Whether you're working in the mailroom or running the whole show, you'll be more effective if you vary your attack on your problems and opportunities. You'll also have more fun, and be less of a bore.

Know how something disappears if you stare at it long enough? And if everybody knows you're going to shout when you stand up, they'll turn off their receivers.

Work can be approached obliquely as well as directly. This is why people should be allowed to work out their own office hours and vacation patterns. Everybody will have a different system of building up a head of steam and then releasing it.

There is a time for engagement and a time for withdrawal. A time to walk around the job. A time to contemplate it—and a time to just laugh at it.

INDUSTRIAL RELATIONS: FIRE THIS WHOLE DEPARTMENT

This all started years ago when some union-hating ancestor of Harrison Gray Otis or Sewell Avery or Henry Ford the First* was advised by his cardiologist not to ever deal directly with the union leaders. This led to the creation of a V.P. of Labor Relations, who later came to be known as V.P. of Industrial Relations.

Under him a whole swarm of people got on the payroll with a vested interest in keeping management and labor sore at each other. In that regard, they have the same goal as the union leadership.

If you get a participative-management effort going in Plant A, make sure you exempt Plant A from being "helped" in its union dealings by the industrial relations department. Otherwise they'll surely sabotage it.

---

*All three of these men were spectacular union haters: Otis with the Los Angeles *Times*, Avery with Montgomery Ward, and Ford with Ford.

INSTITUTION,
ON NOT BECOMING AN

If you ever get a good Theory Y (*see* People) organization going, the problem becomes how to keep it that way.

One good plan is for the chief executive to insist that he must *personally* use every form in the company before it's installed. Like: requisition forms (for pencils, pads, or air tickets), long-distance-telephone-call forms, or personnel department forms. And his secretary can't fill in the form for him.

If some psychiatrist in the personnel department invents a new application form with a whole lot of questions like "How did you feel about your mother?," before it gets used the chief executive has to fill it out . . . completely. This will kill a lot of bad ideas early.

Related to this is a function that you might describe as vice-president in charge of anti-bureaucratization. He must have a loud voice, no fear, and a passionate hatred for institutions and their practices. In addition to his regular duties, it's his job to wander around the company looking for new forms, new staff departments, and new reports. Whenever he finds one that smells like institutionalization, he screams "Horseshit!" at the top of his lungs. And keeps shouting until the new whatever-it-is is killed.

Billy Graham had a man named Grady Wilson who yelled "Horseshit"—however you say that in Baptist—at him whenever he took himself too seriously. Perhaps that's one of the reasons the Graham organization has been so successful. I had a Chairman of the Executive Committee who used to blow a launch-caller at me.* Every chief executive should find someone to perform this function and then make sure he can be fired only for being too polite. Since the leader must lead the battle against institutionalization, it's to the leader that you should look for early signs of losing the war. Is he getting confused about who's God? Polishing up the image instead of greasing the wheels? Preoccupied with the price of the stock? Listening to the public relations department? Short-tempered with honest criticism? Are people hesitating before they tell him? Is he avoiding risks? Playing it safe? Talking to only certain people? Invisible to the rank and file? Hasn't even met some of the new people? Saying the same old magic words but doing something different?

Heartbreaking, isn't it? But he's probably had his five or six years and it's time for a new leader (*see* Wearing Out Your Welcome).

---

*I was also blessed with a colleague who would break me up every now and then with a top-secret epistle beginning along these lines: "Dear Jefe de Oro: With regard to your latest pronunciamento, if you say so, it will be my hourly concern to make it so. But before I sally forth in service of this your latest cause, I must tell you with deep affection and respect that you're full of shit again . . . etc. etc." These epistles batted about .900.

INVESTMENT BANKERS

Like other suppliers of services (CPAs, commercial bankers, cleaning ladies, and lawyers), investment bankers work better if they sense that you aren't married to them. You should try to keep at least one alternate waiting eagerly (or at least waiting) in the wings.

You do this by having a quarterly lunch or dinner with your alternate contact and by supplying him regularly with your monthly figures (if these people can't respect confidences, nobody can).

While working with your current lawyer or banker, you give him every opportunity to do a good job. You are entitled to expect excellence from him. If you don't get it over a period of time, you had best change firms. It is usually easier to change firms than to reshape a relationship that has gone sour (*see* Lawyers Can Be Liabilities).

INVESTORS:
KEEPING THEM INFORMED

They can be a nuisance when things are going well,
but a positive threat to the company's existence when
things have been going badly.

Here's how Lazard Frères handled the problem of
keeping themselves and other investors informed in one
case of a company they controlled. After the monthly
statements were released, a certain partner would
phone and say he was arriving at company headquarters the following morning. On arrival, he would go into
an office by himself with a list of all division and department heads who were expected to be at headquarters that day. If some had planes to catch, that was
noted on his list. He called them in *one at a time* and
asked them any questions he wanted (they had all seen
the same monthly statements because they were circulated freely to them with the caveat that they not be
discussed outside the company). If he asked a question
that could be answered better by someone else on the
list, the questionee might ask to see the list and then
suggest: "Why not ask *him* that question?" Or in some
cases the questionee would have a go at answering anyway. The chief executive was called in for his half hour

or so just like the others. At the end of the day the Lazard partner left.

Within a week at the outside, a triple-spaced memo would arrive and be circulated rapidly to all the people who had been interviewed (or their deputies if they were out of town on that particular day). The report was corrected as to fact (not style) and then sent back to the Lazard partner the same day. He would have it typed up in final form and sent to the directors and investors.

Note that this process only took an hour or less a month from each manager at the company. Also, since everybody at the company who was interviewed read the whole memo, it was an excellent intra-company communications device.

Since the company had a chance to review and modify it before it went to the investors, any promises or deadlines became doubly binding on the people who had made or set them.

Two things about this technique bear watching.

First, the same man* always came every month. He never sent a substitute. So his knowledge and understanding of the company increased geometrically and

---

*He grew up to be Felix Rohatyn, savior of New York City and adviser to the powerful.

his relationships with the individuals became easier and easier.

Second, he was an honest and fair reporter of what he found.

JAPANESE MANAGEMENT

I don't want to hear any more about the superiority of Japanese management. I'm sorry, but I'm sick of it.

Excluding our major and very real weaknesses—the United Autoworkers, the United Steelworkers, the other major unions, and the managements of the giant companies they're helping to destroy—we have a better labor force and better management than Japan.

So let's concentrate on the 80 percent of the work force who aren't members of big labor, and all the managements who will listen.

For us, there is one overriding critical task: to create an environment in each company in which *all* the people feel like using their brains, their hands, their talents, and their skills to help the company become the best at what it does.

The participative ideas which temporarily gave the Japanese our steel, automobile, television set, and calculator markets are *American** ideas. The Japanese

---

*Quality- or Q-circles, which many Americans think of as an essentially Japanese management technique, were invented and used by IBM twenty-five years ago.

learned how to use them—our giant company managements and unions in their arrogance and shortsightedness did not. But don't sell *all* American management short.

The show isn't over until the fat lady sings.

JOB DESCRIPTIONS—
STRAITJACKETS

Great for jobs where the turnover is high and the work is largely repetitive.

Insane for jobs that pay $500 a week or more. Judgment jobs are constantly changing in nature and the good people should be allowed to use their jobs and see how good they are.

At best, a job description freezes the job as the writer understood it at a particular instant in the past. At worst, they're prepared by personnel people who can't write and don't understand the jobs. Then they're not only expensive to prepare and regularly revise, but they're important morale-sappers.

Labor unions have crippled American industry by narrowing job descriptions.

If a crane motor needs changing in a big union shop, you may need a crane machinist to loosen the motor bolts, a motor inspector to disconnect the electric leads, a pipe fitter to disconnect the lube line, and a rigger to take the motor off. All these workers have to bring their own tools and get them staged. Each one has a foreman who may or may not stand around watching. And you may need a leader because you've collected a pretty big gang. What with all the breaks, a job like this could easily take all day.

In a non-union shop, a millwright and an electrician could change a motor in an hour.

If it were my company, I'd be training the millwrights to be electricians and the electricians to be millwrights; and then all of them to be welders. Paying them more for the additional skills would be equitable and worth it to the company, but I believe it would be of secondary importance to the maintenance people themselves. They really enjoy learning how to do more.

To be satisfying, a job should have variety, autonomy, wholeness, and feedback. In other words, no job description.

KEEPING IN TOUCH

One New York City company has an active reception area: pickup, delivery, and sales to walk-in customers.

To give their receptionists a little down time, but mainly to make sure the bosses never forget how to look a customer in the eye and write up a sales ticket, each executive is on a duty roster which gives him or her two hours a month on the reception desk.

Including the president.

KILLING THINGS, V.P. IN CHARGE OF

It's about eleven times as easy to start something as it is to stop something. But ideas are good for a limited time—not forever.*

If Curtis Publishing had had a good V.P. in charge of killing things, the *Saturday Evening Post*, which was a great idea for many years, would have been killed before it ate up all those careers and all that capital.

The internal-combustion engine should long since have been killed and replaced with some form of external-combustion (pollutionless) engine.

General Foods, the AFL-CIO, the Department of Defense, and the Ford Foundation should make it a practice to wipe out their worst product, service, or activity every so often. And I don't mean cutting it back or remodeling it—I mean right between the eyes.

And just to give us all a glimmer of light at the end of the tunnel, how about making it a matter of law that the federal government for the next hundred years will have to kill two old activities for each new one they start?

---

*Dr. Robert Sobel, Associate Professor of History at Hofstra University, says that the British created a civil service job in 1803 calling for a man to stand on the Cliffs of Dover with a spyglass. He was supposed to ring a bell if he saw Napoleon coming. The job was abolished in 1945.

L **LABOR UNIONS**

. . . including civil service and the American Association of University Professors, are a bloody nuisance.

Unionism, say the most idealistic leaders, has deteriorated into a kind of industrial police force that also sells insurance. The labor movement is now a conservative bureaucracy that resists the creative change of the good manager.

If you don't have them, the best way to avoid them is to create a Theory Y environment (*see* People) where your people have a chance to realize their potential (and get recognition for their contribution) in helping the company reach its objectives.

If you already have unions, then deal with them openly and honestly. Abide by their rules. For example, be meticulous about explaining every new benefit to the delegate privately and well in advance. After all, you want your people (union or not) to have the best deal you can give them. Whether the union grabs the credit for each item is completely immaterial. Don't sell your people short—they know. And don't turn your people

over to the union politician by refusing to initiate benefits on the theory that the union will demand more than
you can offer anyway.

LAWYERS CAN BE LIABILITIES

Getting good legal advice is a question of picking the right individual, not the right firm. Usually the best is a young lawyer on the make. Look for a partner, or an about-to-be partner, who hasn't yet brought in any new business.

A good lawyer will give you his home phone, will travel on weekends and work weekends when it's needed, and will carry the corporate seal in his briefcase.

Beware of the lawyer who talks Middle English or statutory paragraph numbers. Though the common law did start before Chaucer, and though Congress does number sections of its output, you need a lawyer to answer questions, not to show off the glories of his trade.

Lawyers take to politics like bears to honey. Other things being equal, try to pick lawyers who are active in politics—particularly if you hire local lawyers in your regional operations (*see* Washington, D.C., Relations with). The best ones won't try or be able to "fix" things. But they're great antennae. Once you're identified as their client, their friends in local and state governments will often talk to them before taking action that affects you.

LEADERSHIP*

To lead the people, walk behind them.
    —LAO-TZU

True leadership must be for the benefit of the followers, not the enrichment of the leaders. In combat, officers eat last.

Most people in big companies today are administered, not led. They are treated as personnel, not people.

Something is happening to our country. We aren't producing leaders like we used to. A new chief executive officer today, exhausted by the climb to the peak, falls down on the mountaintop and goes to sleep.

Where are our corporate Ethan Allens and John Hancocks and Nathanael Greenes, to say nothing of our George Washingtons, Ben Franklins, and Thomas Jeffersons? If we had to get the modern equivalent of our Founding Fathers together today, the first thing they'd do would be to hire Cresap, McCormick, and Paget† to write the Constitution for them.

---

*A leader often plays two parts. First the open-door, always-available decision-maker, the problem-solver and advice-giver; in this part he is ready to run the Xerox or answer the telephone if that's what needs doing. His other role may be that of chief business-getter, and in this capacity, he needs *service*—he should be treated like an emperor—all his people should run to supply his needs. I believe the CEO and his people should understand that these two opposite roles exist, and also everyone should know when the CEO is playing which. When the CEO starts only playing emperor, he needs to be fired (*see* Time to Fire the CEO?).
†Their initials, some say, stand for "Christ! more people!"

I'm afraid leadership is becoming a lost art:

"Most hierarchies are nowadays so cumbered with rules and traditions, and so bound in by public laws, that even high employees do not have to lead anyone anywhere, in the sense of pointing out the direction and setting the pace. They simply follow precedents, obey regulations, and move at the head of the crowd. Such employees lead *only in the sense that* the carved wooden figurehead leads the ship."*

How do you spot a leader? They come in all ages, shapes, sizes, and conditions. Some are poor administrators, some are not overly bright. One clue: since most people per se are mediocre, the true leader can be recognized because, somehow or other, his people consistently turn in superior performances.

"As for the best leaders, the people do not notice their existence. The next best, the people honor and praise. The next, the people fear; and the next, the people hate. . . . When the best leader's work is done the people say, 'We did it ourselves!' "†

The Peter Principle, by Laurence J. Peter and Raymond Hull, New York, Morrow, 1969.
†From Lao-tzu.

LOW COST = LOW STAFF

When there is little staff, the line does the purchasing,* for example. Instead of the purchasing department's preoccupation with manuals and forms, the line people buy what they need, they buy it now, and they buy the right stuff the first time or they correct their mistakes fast.

---

*Many years ago, I was head of the investment department of American Express. At the time, we were enjoying the reputation of being a hot department and I was carrying my resignation around in my pocket. One day, Mr. Cuccinello, who was investing hundreds of millions of dollars of travelers cheque float in short-term securities every day, came to me with the old hand-crank calculator he'd been using. "Can't we afford one of those new nine-hundred-dollar Japanese electronic machines [they now cost nine dollars]?" he wanted to know. As a dutiful manager should, I went to the purchasing department and asked them politely to buy us a calculator. "Is it in your budget?" my purchasing man asked. "No," I said. "I made out my budget last October and I only learned today how much we need this calculator." "If it's not in your budget, you can't have it," he said with finality. "Please sign this," I said, pulling out my resignation. "Why should I sign this?" he asked. "You don't work for me." "Because," I told him, "when I leave here I'm going into the president's office to resign. If he should ask me why I'm resigning, I'm going to tell him because some stupid son of a bitch in the purchasing department won't buy me a machine that would pay for itself in the first three and a half minutes we owned it. If he asks me *which* stupid son of a bitch in the purchasing department, I want to be able to show him your name." We got the calculator.

M MANAGEMENT AND "TOP" MANAGEMENT

"Top" management (the board of directors) is supposed to be a tree full of owls—hooting when management heads into the wrong part of the forest. I'm still unpersuaded they even know where the forest is (*see* Directors, Board of: The Back-Seat Drivers). "Top" management is free-floating and, like Gulliver's flying island Laputa, only occasionally in touch with the real world of the company they're supposed to direct.

In the giant companies, it's an Elysian field where you put your old pros (and a few legacies) to get them out of the way of the young Turks and let them figurehead annual charity drives. It's a pleasant vague world of ceremony and ritual built around the regular board and committee meetings. The chief executive, if he wants to be effective, spends a token* amount of time eating lotus with these Mandarins.

When stripped of the pejorative "top," the word "management" to me means the chief executive officer and all others who have one or more people reporting to them. Their jobs as managers are fundamentally all the same.

---

*Four board meetings a year are infinitely less wearing on your operating and accounting people than twelve.

The best managers think of themselves as playing coaches. They should be the first on the field in the morning and the last to leave it at night. They're available to their players seven days a week from 8 a.m. to 11 p.m. In the business context, being there on the scene and available is a simple necessity—an if-not-forget-it. Timing is everything. If the manager isn't there when he's needed—to supply the blessing or the go-ahead or the missing piece of a puzzle—his people will lose satisfaction, then interest and zeal.

A good manager is a blocking back whenever and wherever needed. No job is too menial for him if it helps one of his players advance toward his objective. How many times has a critical project been held up because there was no one around who could get someone out of bed, or type up a fresh draft, or run off some copies on the Xerox. A good manager carries his players' home phone numbers with him and has an understanding with them that, just as he is available to them until eleven o'clock any night, so they are available to him on the same terms.

Like a good coach, he protects his players from unreasonable demands of the owners. In business, he identifies company objectives and gets his players to see them as their objectives. Then he gets "top" management to agree to the objectives. Once this is done, he is able to be hard-nosed with "top" management whenever they try to distract him or his players.

"Top" managements are easily panicked when the organization is having a lean year. If the chief executive doesn't calm them down, they can blow hither and yon and hot and cold. Under these conditions they must be constantly and forcefully told off when they suggest something or try something that not only doesn't help the chief and his team but actually sets them back.

A good* "top" management should read the monthly reports, meet quarterly with the chief executive, and function as his sounding board. For these duties, they should be paid less than, not more than, key division and department heads. The Establishment in any field seldom earns its pay.

*I must take it on faith that there are good "top" managements. I've just never seen one.

MANAGEMENT CONSULTANTS

The effective ones are the one-man shows. The institutional ones are disastrous. They waste time, cost money, demoralize and distract your best people, and don't solve problems. They are people who borrow your watch to tell you what time it is and then walk off with it.

Don't use them under any circumstances. Not even to keep your stockholders and directors quiet. It isn't worth it.

Many organizations who've been through it will react promptly, thoroughly, and effectively to the threat: "If you fellows don't get shaped up in thirty days so you're a credit to the rest of the company, I'm going to call in McKinsey."

MARKETING

"Marketing" departments—like planning departments, personnel departments, management development departments, advertising departments, and public relations departments—are usually camouflage designed to cover up for lazy or worn-out chief executives.

Marketing, in the fullest sense of the word, is the name of the game. So it had better be handled by the boss and his line, not by staff hecklers. Once or twice a year for three or four days the boss takes ten, twenty, or thirty of his key people, including some from the ad agency and the controller's office, away to some secluded spot. On average they spend twelve hours a day asking unaskable questions, rethinking the business (What are we selling? To whom? At what prices? How do we get it to him? In what form?), four hours a day relaxing and exercising, and eight hours a day sleeping. It's hard work. But more good marketing changes will come out of such meetings than out of any year-round staff department of "experts" with "marketing" signs on the door.

MARS, MAN FROM

In solving a complex problem, pretend that you are a Martian. Assume that you understand everything about Man and his Society—except what has been done in the past by other companies in your industry to solve this particular problem.

For example, when the Massachusetts Turnpike Authority was about to tear down the Avis headquarters in Boston, we asked ourselves, "Where would a man from Mars locate the headquarters of an international company in the business of renting and leasing vehicles without drivers?" The main criteria became clear: near active domestic and international airports, so we could go see our managers and they could get to us; and in a good accounting and clerical labor market. So we moved to Long Island between JFK and La Guardia, while our larger competition isolated itself on the tight little island of Manhattan.

MEETINGS

Generally speaking, the fewer the better. As to both
the number of meetings and the number of participants.

There are several kinds of useful meetings. Here are a
couple:

The Weekly Staff Meeting
Purpose: information, not problem-solving.
For: all division and department heads.
Takes place same time, same place, like TV news.
Starts *on the dot no matter who's missing*.
Goes around the room: reports on problems, develop-
ments (a crossed wire is handled by Joe saying to Pete,
"I'll see you after the meeting on that"). A number of
people should and will say, "Pass."
Ends on the dot (or sooner).
No attendance taken.
No notice of meeting sent in advance.
No stigma for non-attendance.
One-page minutes dictated, typed, *and* circulated the
same day.*

Every six months have a secret ballot—"Do we *need* a
weekly staff meeting?"

---

*The chief ought to write this. In the worst companies, the chief's assistant-to does
it, and undoes all the trust created by the meeting.

The Problem- (or Opportunity-) Focused Meeting

Shouldn't happen more than a few times a year after a company gets going. A good manager with a nose for when an important problem or opportunity is facing his group earns his salt by calling this meeting. In my experience it's really a series of meetings.

After the first session, some are against, some are for, some think it's all a waste of time. I usually try to pick out a well-respected operating man who is reasonably enthusiastic about the idea and pair him with an assistant controller. They are asked to come back in a week to report (orally) to the original group on whether the idea makes sense.

After this second meeting, either the idea is pretty obviously major (so you can ask for a written detailed battle plan to be submitted by your two-man team at the end of another week) or you apologize to the group for wasting time.

Two Meetings Better Than One

Some people absorb ideas quickly from conversation; others respond better to written material. First reactions are best from some people; the next day they're not so sure. Other people shouldn't be rushed.

Once I had a very able and valuable associate who would get negative and defensive if pressed for a decision in the first meeting on anything. He taught me that if it's worth having one meeting on a matter, it's usually worth having a second meeting first thing the next morning. At the first you pick up the convictions of the quick reactors, and at the second you give equal time to the just-as-valuable convictions of those who should sleep on it.

MEMORANDUM, THE LAST*

Use them for dissemination of non-controversial information. Write them to yourself to organize your thoughts. But keep in mind that a memo is really a one-way street. There's no way to reply to it in real time, or to engage it in a dialogue. Murder-by-memo is an acceptable crime in large organizations, and a zealous user of the Xerox machine gun can copy down dozens of otherwise productive people. The small company cannot survive such civil war games.

When two of your departments or divisions start arguing by memo and copying you, call them in and make them swear never to write another memo on that subject. Then listen to both sides, and if they won't work it out then and there, decide it (*see* Compromise and King Solomon). When the conflict between the State and Defense departments was at its peak, it was rumored that 20 percent of the employees of each department were there just to throw memo grenades at the other.

Memos and all other documents should always bear dates and initials. One of my colleagues once spent a twelve-hour night working on an undated document

*"The letter killeth, but the spirit giveth life."—St. Paul

which turned out not to be the current draft. Why he was not convicted of mayhem remains a mystery.

If I were ever again sentenced to run a bank, I promise you one of my first official acts would be to write a memorandum to everybody, beginning, "This is the last memorandum . . ."

MERCY MISPLACED

The average leader avoids prescribing corporate euthanasia for a limping company operation. Why? Not because he can't read the numbers—he's sharp enough with those. Because he came up through a system that excessively rewards the ability to get along with other people.

Mercy may help him get along for the moment. But misplaced mercy is seldom merciful. As a result of his soft-headed decision, bright, able people get trapped in an obsolete division. They bust their humps fighting to salvage a lost cause.

The standard performance-appraisal sheet offers a constant reminder of how far off the track we are with respect to the qualities we need in our leaders. It emphasizes the self-serving skills of the corporate politicians who can't come up with hard decisions that are *truly* merciful in the long run.

"Flexibility," "Adaptability," "Gets along well with others." I don't believe they're what's needed today if we're going to force our institutions to adapt to *us*— which is our central problem.

The Ottoman Turks for over three centuries produced

an unbroken succession of able leaders. Their performance-appraisal sheet would have looked like this:

Adaptability	0
Adventuresomeness	100
Cruelty	100
Energy	100
Flexibility	0
Intelligence	100
Justice	100
Gets along well with others	0

Please note—justice, 100. Without that, they would have been nothing.

May I suggest that if you don't start developing your own Ottoman Turks, pretty soon they'll be coming over your walls?

MERGERS, CONGLOBULATIONS, AND JOINT FAILURES

Joint ventures are almost always bad. At worst, both parents neglect the stepchild in favor of their own. At best, one parent does all the work, but has to give up half the rewards and justifiably begins to feel cheated. The worst kind of joint ventures are those with a supplier-customer relationship between the parents and the joint venture. Someone always ends up being screwed. Do it by yourself if it's worthwhile, and don't do it at all if it's not.

Acquisitions and mergers are a necessary evil for some companies. Avoid them like the plague if you can. If you can't, set up a team separate and distinct from the operating management of your company to handle them. An underworked but talented president, chairman, or Chairman of the Executive Committee plus a talented director from Wall Street make a good combination. Let them work directly with someone assigned by the controller. Make sure that all three understand:

1. *That the business will be run as if no acquisition or merger will ever happen, and*
2. *That no one (including the chief executive officer)*

will ever be disturbed until the deal is in the eleventh hour, and I mean 11:55.

At that point, the chief executive, the affected divisions and departments, and the controller's office can drop everything for forty-eight hours and, having heard about the deal for the first time, either buy it or kill it. But they don't spend a minute a year on the myriad deals that fall apart on the way to the closing.*

If you have a good company, don't sell out to a conglomerate. I was sold out once but resigned (*see* Disobedience and Its Necessity). Conglomerates will promise anything for your people (if your stock sells for a lower multiple of earnings and has a faster earnings growth rate than theirs), but once in the fold your company goes through the homogenizer along with their other acquisitions of the week, and all the zeal and most of the good people leave.

Two and two may seem to make five when a conglomerate is making its pitch, but from what I've seen they are just playing a numbers game and couldn't care less if they make zombies out of your people.

Don't expect lawyers or investment bankers to be objective about conglomerates. Visions of sugar plums dance through their heads at the mention of Gulf and Western or United Technologies.

---

*Of course, your acquisition team should disclose the existence of this veto power before any negotiations get serious. Then they won't be accused of bad faith if you kill a deal at the last minute.

MESSAGE TO CHIEF EXECUTIVES

Probably whenever Sitting Bull, Geronimo, and the other chiefs powwowed, the first topic of conversation was the shortage of Indians. Certainly today, no meeting of the high and the mighty is complete until someone polishes the conventional wisdom: "Our big trouble today is getting enough good people."

This is crystal-clear nonsense. Your people aren't lazy and incompetent. They just look that way. They're beaten by all the overlapping and interlocking policies, rules, and systems encrusting your company.

Do you realize that your people can't make long-distance calls without filling out a report? Do you know what they have to go through to hire somebody—or buy something? Stop running down your people. It's *your* fault they're rusty from underwork. Start tearing down the system where it has defeated and imprisoned them. They'll come to life fast enough. Be the Simón Bolívar of your industry. *Olé!*

MISTAKES

Admit your own mistakes openly, maybe even joyfully.

Encourage your associates to do likewise by commiserating with them. Never castigate. Babies learn to walk by falling down. If you beat a baby every time he falls down, he'll never care much for walking.

My batting average on decisions at Avis was no better than .333. Two out of every three decisions I made were wrong. But my mistakes were discussed openly and most of them corrected with a little help from my friends.

Beware the boss who walks on water and never makes a mistake. Save yourself a lot of grief and seek employment elsewhere.

MISTRESSES

It's interesting that otherwise competent businessmen, capable of budgeting a complex operation, can't figure out that the cost of maintaining two women is twice the cost of one plus certain fringes. An early symptom of the mistress is a sudden surge of creativity in an executive's expense account. I once had a personnel vice-president who had taken up with one of our executive secretaries. If it had been outside the company, I wouldn't have minded unless it interfered with his work. But a personnel man with his arm around an employee is like a treasurer with his hand in the till.

Having nothing but persistent rumors to go on, I was dragging my feet until all of a sudden all the executive secretaries got a raise. ("Thank heavens," somebody said later, "he wasn't sleeping with a key-punch operator.") But how do you get proof? I'm against using shamuses. Finally it came to me. Suppose it were me. Suppose my boss called me in and told me I was fired and why. If I were innocent, I'd go off like a roman candle. If I were guilty, I'd sheepishly ask, "Who did you hear that story from?"

That afternoon I called him in and told him. He lowered his eyes and asked, "Who told you that story?"

He was a good man. I helped him start again a little
way from temptation in another company. When I cut
all the executive secretaries back to their previous
pay levels, not one raised the voice of righteous indig-
nation.

MOONLIGHTING

Like sleeping around, it scatters energy. It usually means that the salary isn't enough to cover living expenses or the psychic income is below the subsistence line. If there's a lot of it going on, it may be a sign that the system has defeated the people again. If they can't release their spare energies toward your goals, they'll moonlight for somebody who doesn't have job descriptions and policy manuals.

MOVING THE HEAD OFFICE

Put one man in charge of the whole operation (let's say
his name is U. Heep), and give him the following
frame of reference:

1. *All executive offices (including the chief's) must be
   the same size (small) and furnished with the same
   basic furniture.*

2. *Don't consult or listen to anyone inside the company
   (especially not the chief executive) on matters of taste
   or preference.*

3. *Hire whatever independent experts you really need.
   But don't ask for advice unless you intend to use it.*

4. *If the building is ready on time, works reasonably
   well, and the cries of outraged vanity and offended
   taste die out within thirty days, it will be named the
   Heep Building. If not, it will be named the Heep
   Memorial Building.*

The usual practice is to hire architects and decorators
and have them report to a committee of tasteless slobs.
After taking twice as long and costing three times as

---

*As anyone knows who has ever moved a head office, it can be very expensive. From
the standpoint of billing cycles and collection of receivables, two moves equal one
fire. My concern with sameness of basic furniture is in deference to the timetable.
Six months after the move, when the business is out of shock, give each officer the
same budget for refurnishing and redecorating and let him run amok if he wants to.
If someone feels that cushions on the floor, psychedelic posters, and black lights will
help him get his job done, I'm all for it. For further philosophy on offices, *see*
Telephone Operators.

much, this method leaves you with one solid result: all your key people are now completely preoccupied with status symbols and have no time for their work.

NEPOTISM, THE SMELL OF

The fatal fact about nepotism is that the really good people won't go to work for you in the first place or will quit or quit trying for your job when they spot your uncle, brother, nephew, wife, mistress, or son on the payroll. They can't expect a fair shake if you're getting breakfast news from a special source.

And what nepotists can't seem to understand is that it doesn't matter whether they're playing family favorites or not. Or even how good the relative is. If there's even a bare possibility that you're prejudiced, the smell of it will scare off or turn off the very people you need most. The stockholders will never know how many good people they missed who never applied for a job.

One odd thing about nepotism is that people with strong Calvinist tendencies are often hardest to persuade. The molecular biologist working long hours for low pay to cure cancer has a relative working as a lab technologist. When questioned, he says, "I'd have to pay twice as much for someone half as good." He misses the point. If his nephew ever cuts a corner because he's thinking of last night's football game or to-night's big date, the rest of the lab staff will catch the infection. To them, he's the boss's nephew.

"But my brother is the best salesman in the business," says the sales manager. Then let him prove it somewhere else. If he's that good, it's not fair to him to stay under you where he'll never know for sure how good he is.

Nepotism is a way of screwing the non-family shareholders. If all the shareholders are family, then it doesn't matter: they're only screwing each other. But when Ford Motor Company stock was sold to the public, Henry II and his brothers should have gotten out of the management. When they didn't, it seemed inevitable that their first classic misadventure should turn out to be named after a relative.

In the old world, nepotism worked fine for the Rothschilds.

It won't work in the new world for anybody.

RCA is still recovering from Bobby Sarnoff.

In rich companies built on an important share of an oligopoly, nepotism may take a while to work its woe. But two or three more generations of Marriotts, Houghtons, and Howard Clarks may well turn strong companies like Marriott Corporation, Corning Glass, and American Express into weaklings.

NO-NO's

Reserved parking spaces. If you're so bloody important, you better be first one in the office. Besides, you'll meet a nice class of people in the employees' parking lot.

Special-quality stationery for the boss and his elite.

Muzak, except in the areas where the work is only suitable for mental defectives.

Bells and buzzers (even telephones can be made to signal with lights).

Company shrinks. Unless it's really optional, and the shrink reports only to the patient, and suitable precautions have been taken to make sure the personnel department can't tap into the data.

Outside directorships and trusteeships for the chief executive. Give up all those non-jobs. You can't even run your own company, dummy.

Company plane. It's just a variation of the company-paid golf club, and the big office with three secretaries. Another line drawn through the company between the Brahmins and the untouchables. And the plane's always in Palm Beach, Augusta, Aspen, or Las Vegas when the business needs it.

Manager's Monthly. Or any other time-consuming report imposed on the troops by "top" management. It's a joke because it consumes ten pounds of energy to produce each ounce of misunderstanding.

Except in poker, bridge, and similar play-period activities,
don't con anybody.
Not your wife
Not your children
Not your employees
Not your customers
Not your stockholders
Not your boss
Not your associates
Not your suppliers
Not your regulatory authorities
Not even your competitors

Don't con yourself either.

Social relations within the firm. Okay with your peers. But not with people who report to you. You'll inevitably see more of the ones you like—and they may not be the best performers. Your own performance depends on your ability to be just. Don't make it any tougher than it is.

Hiring. To keep an organization young and fit, don't

hire anyone until everybody's so overworked they'll be glad to see the newcomer no matter where he sits.

Trade associations—as a chance to fix prices and allocate customers and markets with your friendly competitors. Antitrust laws are different: you're not innocent until proven guilty. If all your customers are north of Main Street and all your competitor's customers are south of Main Street, you're both guilty by inference. And nobody has to prove the two of you ever communicated in any way. Treble damages. Jail. So watch it, bubele.

Conventions. The public relations dream: much money, time, and energy signifying nothing. The best way is to ignore them. The next-best way is to send one line man (rotate the assignment like kitchen police). On his return, ask him to make a thirty-second all-inclusive oral report to the weekly staff meeting covering everything of significance that he heard, saw, and learned. The worst way is to give your P.R. department a blank check and tell them to make a big splash.

House organs. Spend the money making stockholders out of your employees and then sending them (along with the other stockholders) honest reports on how the company's really doing: good and bad. Reading a house organ is like going down in warm maple syrup for the third time.

Pension plans for top people. Security is for people who don't have a chance to make it big. Above a certain level (you pick it), don't have pensions. Encourage your people to build their own security by building the company they own a piece of.

Taking phone calls in meetings: "Look at me, I'm busy!" If you get a phone call from the President of the United States, how much more impressive *not* to take it. Besides, your refusal will strike panic into those nineteen Medusas on the White House switchboard, who believe they have the divine right to interrupt anybody, anywhere, anytime.

Tax dodges. Don't encourage your people—with company cars and company apartments—to take their eyes off profit building and focus on tax-saving schemes instead.

Synergism, a business fad like hula hoops, holds that two and two makes five. Horseshit. Two and two usually makes three, and you know it. Because divisions forced to deal with one another learn to hate with a passion—and find ways to take it out on one another.

Consistency is something you have to be inconsistent about. With a nationwide franchise agreement, be consistent; if you permit one variation, the finger is out of the dike. But where the advantages far outweigh the disadvantages—such as letting people set their own of-fice hours and firing those who consistently abuse that freedom—you must be consistently inconsistent.

Liquor and drugs. Don't try to tell people how to conduct themselves at home. But if someone comes to the office zonked a third time, fire him without bother-ing to find out what he's using.

Greed. To increase our share of the market a few years ago, I was on the verge of approving the start-up of a new subsidiary—which would compete with our bread-and-butter business—at discount prices. To ver-ify my own brilliance I tried the idea out on a tall, rangy regional vice-president named Stepnowski. After hearing the plan described in some detail, he sank the whole project with one sentence: "I don't know what *you* call it, but we Polacks call that 'pissing in the soup.' "

OBJECTIVES

One of the important functions of a leader is to make the organization concentrate on its objectives. In the case of Avis, it took us six months to define one objective—which turned out to be: "We want to become the fastest-growing company with the highest profit margin in the business of renting and leasing vehicles without drivers."

That objective was simple enough so that we didn't have to write it down. We could put it in every speech and talk about it wherever we went. And it had some social significance, because up to that time Hertz had a crushingly large share of the market and was thinking and acting like General Motors.

It also included a definition of our business: "renting and leasing vehicles without drivers." This let us put the blinders on ourselves and stop considering the acquisition of related businesses like motels, hotels, airlines, and travel agencies. It also showed us that we had to get rid of some limousine and sightseeing companies that we already owned.

Once these objectives are agreed on, the leader must be merciless on himself and on his people. If an idea that pops into his head or out of their mouths is outside the objective of the company, he kills it without a trial.

Peter Drucker was never more right than when he wrote:

*"Concentration is the key to economic results . . . no other principle of effectiveness is violated as constantly today as the basic principle of concentration . . . Our motto seems to be: 'Let's do a little bit of everything.' "**

It isn't easy to concentrate. I used to keep a sign opposite my desk where I couldn't miss it if I was on the telephone (about to make an appointment) or in a meeting in my office: "Is what I'm doing or about to do getting us closer to our objective?" That sign saved me from a lot of useless trips, lunch dates, conferences, junkets, and meetings.

Most of all, work on simplifying and distilling your statement of objectives. Cato boiled his down to three words†—and by saying them over and over eventually wiped out the competition.

---

*Managing for Results, New York, Harper & Row, 1964.
†Lest we forget, the words were: *Delenda est Carthago*.

OFFICE PARTY, HOW
NOT TO DO THE ANNUAL

1. *Start it at 5 p.m. instead of noon, so the company doesn't lose any man-hours.*
2. *Invite spouses so bosses and their secretaries don't enjoy dancing together.*
3. *Make sure the top brass either doesn't show or puts in a token appearance—underscoring the difference between them and the rest of us playful, indolent darkies.*
4. *Invite clients and suppliers to help reinforce their contempt for your company.*
5. *Skimp on the setting. A third-rate roadhouse is always good.*
6. *Cut corners on the food and booze. Two-day-old hors d'oeuvres left over from a wedding, a tray of manhattans, and a mystery punch ought to do it.*
7. *Save money on the music. Better than a phonograph is a tin-eared accordionist whose idea of a new number is "I Could Have Danced All Night."*
8. *Kill two birds by combining it with the annual quarter-century-club party. Then all your employees can see living examples (you should excuse the expression) of what twenty-five years in your outfit will do to what were once healthy human beings.*

9. *Better yet, turn the whole thing over to the head of the personnel department and tell him to use his best judgment.*

ORGANIZATION CHARTS: RIGOR MORTIS

They have uses: for the annual salary review; for educating investors on how the organization works and who does what.

But draw them in pencil. Never formalize, print, and circulate them. Good organizations are living bodies that grow new muscles to meet challenges. A chart demoralizes people. Nobody thinks of himself as *below** other people. And in a good company he isn't. Yet on paper there it is. If you have to circulate something, use a loose-leaf table of organization (like a magazine masthead) instead of a diagram with the people in little boxes. Use alphabetical order by name and by function wherever possible.

In the best organizations, people see themselves working in a circle as if around one table. One of the positions is designated chief executive officer, because somebody has to make all those tactical decisions that enable an organization to keep working. In this circular organization, leadership passes from one to another depending on the particular task being attacked—without any hang-ups.

This is as it should be. In the hierarchical organiza-

---

*20th Century–Fox used the length of line between boxes to measure progress up the organization.

tion, it is difficult to imagine leadership anywhere but at the top of the various pyramids. And it's hard to visualize the leader of a small pyramid becoming temporarily the leader of a group of larger pyramid-leaders which includes the chief executive officer.

The traditional organization chart has one dead giveaway. Any dotted line indicates a troublemaker and/or a serious troubled relationship. It also generally means that an unsatisfactory compromise (*see* Compromise and King Solomon) has been worked out and the direct solution has been avoided.

PAPER TIGERS

Printed forms for performance appraisals and MBOs (management by objective) are used by incompetent bosses in badly managed companies.

Real managers manage by frequent eyeball contact. "Half our meetings are held in the hall, the other half in the washroom," says one good manager.

Once I worked as a consultant for Alan Ladd, Jr., who ran the pictures division of 20th Century–Fox. Laddie's boss was Dennis Stanfill, a stiff, straitlaced, by-the-book chief executive who communicated by memo and formal meeting. Laddie's division was very relaxed, and Laddie communicated by smiles, slight frowns, eyebrow twitches, and occasional grunts. Memos he didn't read (he took them home for daughter Amanda to use for paper airplanes—that way they didn't clutter up his files).

When I was hired, the top forty people in the division were groaning through the semiannual MBO process. "What five or six objectives will you accomplish in the next six months and what percentage of your time will you spend on each?" After these forms were filled out

with much nagging from corporate staff, they were read
and signed by each superior and sent back to corporate, who rewrote them into acceptable gobbledygook
and returned them for re-signature (nobody ever questioned the rewrites). This process took about six
months, and just as everybody was heaving a sigh and
going back to work, back would come the "How did
you do compared to what you said you were going to
do?" forms.

The corporate staff was making a nonsense out of an
essential part of management. In a well-managed company, plans are made and promises of action by certain
dates are being extracted (MBO, no?) in the parking lot
and in the cafeteria all the time, not just twice a year.

When I couldn't get Dennis to stop the program, I persuaded him to accept simple statements *not on forms,*
and to stop his storm troopers from rewriting them.
Back in the division, I offered to write everybody's
MBOs. About two-thirds (including Laddie) took me up
on it and the whole process took about a week twice a
year. Much too much time for what it accomplished
(fear and loathing of corporate), but better than before.

PARTICIPATIVE MANAGEMENT: DO YOU REALLY HAVE AN ENLIGHTENED COMPANY?

For the last fourteen years I've been plagued by CEOs claiming to run enlightened Theory Y (*see* People) companies. Without exception, every one I've visited has been a Theory X nightmare. It seems I haven't been approached by anybody *really* running a good show because they're all too busy and having too much fun.

Here's a quiz. If you score 9 or 10, I'd like to come visit you.

Good or **Bad**

_____ *Communication. Visible leaders listening to workers. Informal atmosphere. A good ask/ listen mechanism (see Suggestion Boxes: Make Them into Birdhouses).*

_____ *Meetings. Answer* GOOD *if you have few scheduled.*

_____ *Policy manuals. Answer* GOOD *if you don't have any.*

_____ *Profit sharing. President to janitor.*

_____ *Salaried employees. President to janitor.*

> *If an assembler is home sick, she gets paid too.*

_____ **Secrecy.** *Answer* GOOD *if salary information is available to anyone and if financial reports are given to all superintendents and openly discussed throughout the company.*

_____ **Staff.** *Minimal. Line people do the hiring, training, purchasing, systems redesign, and so forth.*

_____ **Structure.** *Shallow. The best companies get along with five levels of management. If you have more than six from CEO to sweeper, answer* BAD.

_____ **Time clocks.** *Answer* GOOD *if you don't have them.*

_____ **Training.** *People get more pay for learning other jobs and skills after they've mastered their own.*

PEOPLE

There's nothing fundamentally wrong with our country except that the leaders of all our major organizations are operating on the wrong assumptions.* We're in this mess because for the last two hundred years we've been using the Catholic Church and Caesar's legions as our patterns for creating organizations. And until the last forty or fifty years it made sense. The average church-goer, soldier, and factory worker was uneducated and dependent on orders from above. And authority carried considerable weight because disobedience brought the death penalty or its equivalent.†

From the behavior of people in these early industrial organizations we arrived at the following assumptions,‡ on which all big organizations are still operating:

1. *People hate work.*
2. *They have to be driven and threatened with punishment to get them to work toward organizational objectives.*
3. *They like security, aren't ambitious, want to be told what to do, dislike responsibility.*

You don't think we are operating on these assumptions? Consider:

---

*By all the evidence, the other industrialized countries except Japan are as badly off, but no worse; their major institutions are operated on the same silly assumptions.
†Dismissal and blacklisting brought starvation to an industrial worker; excommunication brought the spiritual equivalent of death to a churchgoer.
‡Douglas McGregor (in *The Human Side of Enterprise,* New York, McGraw-Hill, 1960) called these three assumptions "Theory X." Organizations that run on these premises—the hierarchies—are Theory X outfits.

1. *Office hours nine to five for everybody except the fattest cats at the top. Just a giant cheap time clock. (Are we buying brains or hours?)*
2. *Unilateral promotions. For more money and a bigger title I'm expected to jump at the chance to move my family to New York City. I run away from the friends and a life style in Denver that have made me and my family happy and effective. (Organization comes first; individuals must sacrifice themselves to its demands.)*
3. *Hundreds of millions of dollars are spent annually "communicating" with employees. The message always boils down to: "Work hard, obey orders. We'll take care of you." (That message is obsolete by fifty years and wasn't very promising then.)*

Back off a minute. Let's pretend we know everything man knows about human nature and its present condition here, but nothing about man's organizations and the assumptions on which they're based. These things* we know about man:

1. *He's a wanting animal.*
2. *His behavior is determined by unsatisfied needs that he wants to satisfy.*
3. *His needs form a value hierarchy that is internal, not external:*
   (a) body (I can't breathe.)

*McGregor again.

(b) safety (How can I protect myself from . . . ?)
(c) social (I want to belong.)
(d) ego (1. Gee, I'm terrific. 2. Aren't I? Yes.)
(e) development (Gee, I'm better than I was last year.)

Man is totally motivated by each level of need in order—until that level is satisfied. If he hasn't slept in three days, he's totally motivated by a need for sleep. After he has slept, eaten, drunk, is safe, and has acceptance in a group, he is no longer motivated by those three levels of needs. (McGregor's examples: The only time you think of air is when you are deprived of it; man lives by bread alone when there is no bread.)

We know that these first three need levels are pretty well satisfied* in America's work force today. So we would expect man's organizations to be designed to feed the ego and development needs. But there's the whole problem. The result of our outmoded organizations is that we're still acting as if people were uneducated peasants. Much of the work done today would be more suitable for young children or mental defectives.

And look at the rewards we're offering our people today: higher wages, medical benefits, vacations, pensions, profit sharing, gymnasiums, swimming pools, bowling and baseball teams. *Not one can be enjoyed on*

---

*This book does not come to grips with the problem of America's 38 million poor: it deals with the 102 million psychiatric cases who do have jobs, whether they're poor or not.

the job. You've got to leave work, get sick, or retire first. No wonder people aren't having fun on the job.

So what are the valid assumptions for present-day circumstances? McGregor called them "Theory Y":

1. *People* don't *hate work. It's as natural as rest or play*.
2. *They don't* have *to be forced or threatened. If they commit themselves to mutual objectives, they'll drive themselves more effectively than you can drive them*.
3. *But they'll commit themselves only to the extent they can see ways of satisfying their ego and development needs (remember, the others are pretty well satisfied and are no longer prime drives)*.

All you have to do is look around you to see that big organizations are only getting people to use about 20 percent—the lower fifth—of their capacities. And the painful part is that God didn't design the human animal to function at 20 percent. At that pace it develops enough malfunctions to cause a permanent shortage of psychoanalysts and hospital beds.

Since 1952 I've been stumbling around building and running primitive Theory Y departments, divisions, and finally one whole Theory Y company: Avis.

In 1962, after thirteen years, Avis had never made a profit.* Three years later the company had grown internally (not by acquisitions) from $30 million in sales to $75 million in sales, and had made successive annual profits of $1 million, $3 million, and $5 million. If I had anything to do with this, I ascribe it all to my application of Theory Y. And a faltering, stumbling, groping, mistake-ridden application it was.

You want proof? I can't give it to you. But let me tell you a story. When I became head of Avis I was assured that no one at headquarters was any good, and that my first job was to start recruiting a whole new team. Three years later, Hal Geneen, the president of ITT (which had just acquired Avis), after meeting everybody and listening to them in action for a day, said, "I've never seen such depth of management; why, I've already spotted three chief executive officers!" You guessed it. Same people. I'd brought in only two new people, a lawyer and an accountant.

Bill Bernbach used to say about advertising effectiveness: "Ninety percent of the battle is what you say and ten percent is what medium you say it in." The same thing is true of people. Why spend all that money and time on the *selection* of people when the people you've got are breaking down from under-use.

---

*Except one year when they jiggled their depreciation rates.

Get to know your people. What they do well, what they enjoy doing, what their weaknesses and strengths are, and what they want and need to get from their job. And then try to create an organization around your people, not jam your people into those organization-chart rectangles. Organizations work when they maximize the chance that each one, working with others, will get for growth in his job. You can't motivate people. That door is locked from the inside. You *can* create a climate in which most of your people will motivate themselves to help the company reach its objectives. Like it or not, the only practical act is to adopt participative-management assumptions and get going.

It isn't easy, but what you're really trying to do is come between a man and his family. You want him to enjoy his work so much he comes in on Saturday instead of playing golf or cutting the grass.

Theory Y is the explanation for Ho Chi Minh's unbelievable twenty-five-year survival against the mighty blasts of Theory X monsters of three nations:

There is nothing to distinguish their generals from their private soldiers except the star they wear on their collars. Their uniform is cut out of the same material, they wear the same boots, their cork helmets are identical and their colonels go on foot like privates. They live on the rice they carry on them, on the tubers they pull out of *the forest earth, on the fish they catch and on the water of the mountain streams. No beautiful secretaries, no prepackaged rations, no cars or fluttering pennants . . . no military bands. But victory, damn it, victory!**

The Battle of Dienbienphu, by Jules Roy, New York, Harper & Row, 1965.

PERSONNEL (PEOPLE VS.)

Fire the whole personnel department.

Unless your company is too large (in which case break it up into autonomous parts), have a one-person people department (not a personnel department). Records can be kept in the payroll section of the accounting department, and your one-person people department acts as personnel (sorry—people) assistant to anybody who is recruiting*—lines up applicants, checks references, and keeps your pay ranges competitive by checking other companies.

On the subject of pay ranges, I've long held the conviction that it's much less expensive to recruit from the top of the barrel by paying top wages. Yet many big personnel departments in insurance companies, banks, and the like consciously recruit from the lower half of the barrel to "save money." If they only realized what they were doing to themselves.

The trouble with personnel experts is that they use gimmicks borrowed from manufacturing: inventories, replacement charts, recruiting, selecting, indoctrinating and training machinery, job rotation, and appraisal programs. And this manufacturing of people is about as effective as Dr. Frankenstein was. As McGregor points

---

*The important thing about hiring is the chemistry or the vibrations between boss and candidate: good, bad, or not there at all.

out, the sounder approach is agricultural. Provide the climate and proper nourishment and let the people grow themselves. They'll amaze you.

PLANNING, LONG-RANGE: A HAPPENING

Planning is best handled by the boss and his key people (*see* Marketing, *for how*).

Once I was asked to head up a new long-range planning effort. My wife listened to my glowing description of my new job. Next evening she blew the whole schmeer out of the water by asking: "What did you plan today, dear?" Bless her.

POLAROID POWER

If you're responsible for a group of hamburger stands, service stations, banks, nursing homes, or supermarkets, where appearance is critical, take a Polaroid camera along on your trips. If you see an obsolete sign, a dirty counter, or a slovenly employee, take a picture. Show it to the manager. Tell him it will be prominently featured in your rogues' gallery back home until he sends you a picture of the new look.

Worth a thousand words? More like a million.

POLICY MANUALS

Don't bother. If they're general, they're useless. If they're specific, they're how-to manuals—expensive to prepare and revise.

The only people who read policy manuals are gold-bricks and martinets. The goldbricks memorize them so they can say: (a) "That's not in this department" or (2) "It's against company policy." The martinets use policy manuals to confine, frustrate, punish, and eventually drive out of the organization every imaginative, creative, adventuresome woman and man.

If you *have* to have a policy manual, publish the Ten Commandments.

POLICY MANUALS: A VIGNETTE

A friend of mine had a chance to start a business from scratch.

"We'll have a policy of no policies," he said to his nucleus team.

"Like what?" asked one.

"Well, I don't believe in a dress code," he said.

"Great," said another. "Let's have a policy of no neckties!"

"No," said my friend. "We'll have a policy of no policies. If we had a policy of no neckties, I'd have to wear a necktie to work from then on!"

P.R. DEPARTMENT, ABOLITION OF

Yes, fire this whole department, too. If you have an outside P.R. firm, fire them.

Most businesses have a normal P.R. operation: press releases, clipping services, attempts to get interviewed; all being handled, as usual, by people who are embarrassingly uninformed about the company's plans and objectives.

We made many mistakes at Avis, but we were at least smart enough to realize that the professional P.R. operation was as dead as the button-hook industry. We knew too many editors had trigger mechanisms that acted automatically to wastebasket anything starting off: "For release."

So we eliminated the P.R. staff. And we called in the top ten or so people in the company and the telephone operators and told them they were the P.R. department.

The telephone operators were given the home phones of the ten people and asked to find one of them if any of the working press called with a question.

The ten people were given the following framework within which they could be themselves and talk freely:

1. *Be honest. If you don't know, say so. If you know but won't tell, say so.*
2. *Pretend your ablest competitor is listening. If he already knows your latest marketing plan, you use the call to announce it; if not, shut up. (This mind-set also prevents knocking the competition, which is always bad for everybody.)*
3. *Don't forecast earnings. If asked why not, tell them we don't do in public anything we can't do consistently well (and believe me, nobody can forecast earnings consistently well).*

This system worked well.* Example: One day Ford Motor Company announced they were going directly into the rent a car business through any Ford dealer that wanted to. The *Wall Street Journal* phoned and was put through to the general manager of our rent a car division. Next day the front-page left-hand column was heavily salted with quotes from their conversation.

Far down the page our competitor's V.P. of public relations had pulled off this coup: "A spokesman for the Hertz Corporation said they were studying the matter."

Hertz was older and twice our size, but who looked like the industry leader that morning?

---

*It also worked with security analysts and portfolio managers who wanted to come see us. When one telephoned for an appointment, I'd give him the rules: "Our next session [we had about one a month] is on April 10. It lasts from ten to four. There'll be three or four other analysts present. We'll give you our board room and you can call in whoever's around of our top ten people one at a time." Not one liked the idea at first. But each one admitted later that he'd learned from the other questions. And each had been impressed by the openness and competence of our people. Yet the time consumed by us was less than forty-five minutes per Avis executive per month.

PRESIDENT'S SALARY (IS HE REALLY WORTH $750,000?)

Every couple of years at an otherwise routine board meeting, some outside director asks your chief executive to leave the room.* Then he mumbles something about underpaid and proposes a raise to $750,000 a year, which is unanimously approved.†

During the months that follow, the chief proposes raises for his various top officers, and when the process is complete, they are all nicely in line with each other and with the average relationship between top officers' salaries of all large, medium, or small corporations as compiled and published by the National Industrial Conference Board.

Over the years a sizable and unjustifiable salary gaposis develops between that privileged group and the people who are doing the real work.

Pick out the workers in your company whose knowledge or experience gets you from January to December. Which people could really hurt by going over to the competition? Your board of directors? Your vice-chairman? Hell, no! If they joined your competitor en masse, you'd be fourteen lengths ahead in a year, con-

---

*Chances are your chief executive sits on his board and does the same for him.
†This whole procedure defies a sound principle: "Board meetings (or any other silly ritual) should be conducted as if Ralph Nader were present by invitation."

sidering your lightened load and your competitor's added burden.

Your key resource people may be engineers, designers, artists, city managers, accountants, mathematicians, chemists, editors, district sales managers, or some of each. But average them all out and they're making one-fifth of what the chief executive gets.

Fair? Not in my book. And it cuts two ways.

The salary gap makes the key people frustrated and restless. And as the chief's salary edges up out of the earth's atmosphere, one of two reactions sets in. Sub-consciously or consciously impressed by how much he is paid, he either becomes:

1. *Arrogant (since I'm so good, I'd better see that all important decisions get the laying on of hands in my office before they're made). The company grinds to a halt and the zeal drains out.*
   or
2. *Timid (I'm paid this much to make sure nothing goes wrong, so I'd better have a look at everything before it happens). The company grinds to a halt and the zeal drains out.*

Why does the chief executive permit this gaposis, which is so bad for the company? I guess because he hasn't thought it through. It certainly can't be the money. He doesn't get to keep it. He's just a conduit between his own stockholders and the Internal Revenue Service.

Gaposis can be fought.

When André Meyer hired me to run Avis twenty years ago, the last item he covered was my salary. "You'll be paid $50,000."

"No I won't," said I. "As an about-to-be-substantial stockholder I insist the president be paid $36,000 because that's top salary for a company that has never earned a nickel for its stockholders."

"D'accord," said André, who always knew when to give up.

When Avis moved into the black a year later, General Sarnoff, one of our outside directors, asked me to leave the room. "I'd prefer not to," I said.

"Why not?" he asked.

"Because if I do you'll raise my salary. And since I'm now overpaid* in relation to the service agents, rental agents, city managers, and regional vice-presidents who run this company, you'll be defeating my crusade for a just compensation system. And since fifteen percent of the pre-tax profits goes into a profit-sharing fund for the

---

*I was still making $36,000.

top five hundred people, that raise will come out of their pockets, and if I were them I wouldn't like it."

The General never liked to be crossed, and I'm not sure he ever forgave me. But he learned so much about the rent a car business on the Avis board that soon after Avis was sold to ITT, he bought Hertz for RCA. Come to think of it, we should have charged him tuition fees.

Ideally, a new chief executive should negotiate his own compensation on a once-and-for-all basis before he goes to work. That is, he may get fired at any time, but if things go well, he gets no more goodies except those that flow from the success of the enterprise (stock appreciation, for example). This puts him in the position of dividing the spoils objectively among his teammates. If he is the divider and a recipient, his directors and stockholders will usually prevail on him to allocate himself more than he deserves.

PROMISES

Keep them. If asked when you can deliver something, ask for time to think. Build in a margin of safety. Name a date. Then deliver it earlier than you promised.

The world is divided into two classes of people: the few people who make good on their promises (even if they don't promise as much) and the many who don't. Get in column A and stay there. You'll be very valuable wherever you are.

You might suppose that the higher you go in the ranks of business executives, the more word-keepers you find. My experience doesn't substantiate this. I've been welshed on by a big bank president, the number-two man of a major finance company, and various investment banking house partners. I only know four people in the business world who I'm sure won't break their word at any price.*

---

*You remember the old story about the philosopher who asked a beautiful socialite at a cocktail party if she would sleep with him for $5 million. She said she would. He asked, "How about $5?" She was outraged. "What do you think I am—a whore?" "We've already established that," said the philosopher, "now I'm trying to establish your price."

PROMOTION, FROM WITHIN

Most managements complain about the lack of able people and go outside to fill key positions. Nonsense. Nobody inside an organization ever looked ready to move into a bigger job.

I use the rule of 50 percent. Try to find somebody inside the company with a record of success (in any area) and with an appetite for the job. If he looks like 50 percent of what you need, give him the job. In six months he'll have grown the other 50 percent and everybody will be satisfied.

How to do it wrong: go outside and get some expensive guy* who looks like 110 percent of what you want and a year later, after having raised salaries all around him, you'll still be teaching him the business. The people around him will be frustrated and ineffective.

One of the keys is to pick someone within the company who has a well-deserved reputation as a winner. Not someone who looks to you like a *potential* winner but doesn't happen to be fitting in very well where he is.

The organization will rally around an accepted winner, even when he's temporarily over his head, because in

---

*Like Maurice Valente, the ITT hotshot who became president and COO of RCA in November 1979 and then, within a year, sank without a trace, taking the CEO, Edgar Griffiths, with him.

their eyes he deserves the chance. The phony who conned you into giving him the job will go down for the third time and pull down everybody else he can reach.

PUBLIC ACCOUNTANTS
AND THE AUDIT COMMITTEE

With the controller's full understanding and agreement, the first time the chief executive meets with his outside auditing team (including the partner in charge) he should say something like this: "We want our accounts to be honest and to give a fair picture of our performance. No matter how bad. Here's a letter from me asking you to report promptly to the audit committee of the board any attempt on my part or anyone else's to influence you otherwise." Then he should ask the auditors to be forthright in their audit report. Too often, problems in an early stage may be only hinted at.

Public accounting firms are expensive. Partners are billed around $145 an hour, managers around $115 an hour, seniors around $75 an hour. Your audit bill will be lower if you encourage the controller to get as much of the routine work done in house before those big meters start ticking.

Ad agencies love to spend your money on market research, and lawyers on legal research. CPA firms will have systems departments and it doesn't take much to start them doing systems work. With all three groups it is well to set up some kind of general alarm that goes off before you accidentally discover they've spent a lot of your money doing work you don't want done.

The audit committee should be two or three independent outside directors. Four is a bull session, one's not enough. They should meet with the outside auditors after the annual audit report comes out, but at least a week before the board of directors meeting to which they will report.

They invite members of management (including the chief executive) at their pleasure into and out of the meeting. Alone with the auditors, they can and should ask questions that would be embarrassing at other times during the year: "Has anyone pressed you to do anything you're reluctant to do?" "Is there any subject or incident that for any reason you didn't include or didn't give proper weight to in the audit report that you'd like to discuss orally now?"

When the audit committee is satisfied that all material questions have been asked, and honest answers given (whether favorable or unfavorable), they are ready to report to the board of directors.

PURCHASING DEPARTMENT

Yes, fire the whole purchasing department.

They cost ten dollars in zeal for every dollar they save through purchasing acumen.

And that doesn't count the massive unrecorded disasters they cause. Let's say somebody has persuaded a young Edison or Steinmetz to go to work for General Conglobulation, Inc. By the time he's found out that there's no way to get that $3,000 personal computer through the purchasing department, he's lost all respect for General Conglobulation. ("They'd hire Einstein and then turn down his requisition for a blackboard.")

So let's be sensible. Fire the whole purchasing department. The company will benefit from having each department dealing in the free market outside instead of being victimized by internal socialism.* And don't underestimate the morale value of letting your people "waste" some money. If you must, have a one-person "buying department" (*see* Personnel [People vs.] for the parallel idea of a one-person people department) for those who want help in the purchasing area and ask for it.

---

*I'm told that the federal government, with all its joint-use purchasing economies, really pays 20 percent more for a pencil than you do at the five-and-ten.

PUTTING ON WEIGHT

A sure sign of frustration is putting on weight. Watch for it on the people who work for you. Remove the cause and the weight will come back off.

R RACISM

Let's face it. The vast majority of corporations are still operating with dice loaded against Jews, blacks, and women of all races and creeds.

Well, it must be clear by now to everybody in touch with reality that it's time to unload the dice. This has to start with a conviction in the chief executive officer. But if he wants more than a scurry by each division to find a token black,* he'd better follow up his bulletin as far down the line as he can and for as long as he is chief executive. Stamping out racism will be a process, not an act, and the chief resistance will be in the personnel office. It is results, not explanations, that count, as in other business action, and you can waste a lot of time just talking.

---

*Things are looking up. You don't hear about the company "nigger" much anymore, and the company "kike" is now the company Jew. Women are still bottom-of-the-heap: "Don't give her a raise; she's making a lot *for a woman*."

REORGANIZING

Should be undergone about as often as major surgery. And should be as well planned and as swiftly executed.

*"I was to learn later in life that we tend to meet any new situation by reorganizing; and a wonderful method it can be for creating the illusion of progress while producing confusion, inefficiency, and demoralization."**

*From Petronius Arbiter (circa A.D. 60).

RETIREMENT, MANDATORY

A sound idea for now. But it can be carried too far.
About ten years ago, American Express put through
automatic across-the-board retirement at age sixty-five.
Their travel competitors threw their caps in the air.
Seems that certain tour guides, like '45, '59, and '61
wines from the great vineyards of Bordeaux, get better
with age. So I'd exempt specialists who have no other
people reporting to them.

Early retirement is also sound, to take care of people
who, like '51 and '54 vintages, didn't work out.

More important than either is to retire the chief executive every five or six years (*see* Wearing Out Your Welcome).

SABBATICALS: STAYING FRESH

For top management or upper-level professionals, this is easy to do. After a successful acquisition, the investment banker goes to Vail or Palm Springs to unwind.

Project-minded companies can refresh their top people the same way.

But in the bump, clunk, and whir industries, that's not where the system fails. The breakdown starts at the foreman level. Typically they start scared, learn the job fast, then get bored and pass the feeling to their men.

One way to beat that is to have five foremen for every four turns. By rotation, one foreman is available each thirty days to work on projects with the general foreman, superintendent, or even top management. This is a sort of working sabbatical.

When he goes back to his turn, his filter is backwashed and he passes his enthusiasm along to his people.

SALARY REVIEW: ANNUAL ENCOUNTER GROUP

Once a year the chief executive officer should review all the salaries of the people reporting to him for relative fairness (not performance). Then he calls in all those people and together they review the salaries of all the people reporting to them in the same light. It's an uncomfortable meeting, but it's only once a year. And by doing it all out in the open you compensate for the fact that some bosses are better salesmen for their people than others.

If this is done right, you can honestly say to people reporting to you who bug you about salary in between annual reviews: "Look, everybody is always either overpaid or underpaid. Let *me* worry about you. If *you* worry about you, you'll be less effective and earn less than you should. Concentrate on your job and look up after every salary review to see if you are being fairly treated."

SALESMEN

1. *Twenty percent of any given group of salesmen will always produce 80 percent of the sales.*
2. *A good incentive-compensation scale for salesmen slides up: 5 percent on the first $100,000 in sales, 7½ percent on the second $100,000, and so forth. And don't modify it if some hot salesman brings down the chandeliers and earns a fortune. That's what you wanted, dummy. The word will go through the sales grapevine and you won't believe the results.*
3. *Top salesmen (all salesmen if you can work it) should be given stock options and encouraged to think like owners.*
4. *A good way to kill a top salesman is to promote him to assistant sales manager.* A manager is one breed, a salesman is another. Most good salesmen thrive in the field, wither at headquarters. "There I was alone," a true salesman once said, "with nothing but my golden voice."*

---

*A viable theory is the Peter Principle: "In a hierarchy, every employee tends to rise to his level of incompetence (the cream rises until it sours)." Peter's corollary: "In time every post tends to be occupied by an employee who is incompetent to carry out its duties." From *The Peter Principle*, by Laurence J. Peter and Raymond Hull, New York, Morrow, 1969.

SCANLON PLAN

Named after Joe Scanlon, steelworker, accountant, steel union president, and popularizer of the idea, it's a plan whereby some simple measure of costs is agreed to as "normal" for a particular company or plant, and 75 percent of any cost reductions resulting from worker suggestions is paid to *all the workers* in monthly bonuses. For more, read *The Scanlon Plan*, edited by Frederick G. Lesieur, Cambridge, MIT Press, 1958.

Let's say you want to try it in one division with 500 people and $25 million in sales; any unit under 3,000 people is workable.

Here's what I'd do.

Make sure you insulate that division from the corporate line and staff people who are threatened by the idea.

Interview several companies with successful Scanlons.

Pick one who will indoctrinate your team. Donnelly Mirrors, Inc., used to do it for $3,000 plus expenses.

Take your top people to an all-day seminar with your teacher-company. Be sure to take the CEO and any high-level skeptics. Donnelly used to give an overview and summary in the morning and then one-on-one meetings with counterparts in the afternoon.

Assuming the CEO and most of the rest are walking on air, get the controller to work out your special tailor-made Scanlon formula and get the approval of the board of directors.

Now take about a fifteen-person cross section of your company, including engineers, foremen, production workers, maintenance people, and secretaries, over to the teacher-company. Same seminar; same one-on-one with counterparts in the afternoon.

Now go back and put it into effect. Build in monthly bonuses rather than quarterly or annual. Post "Howe-doin?" results frequently. Post handwritten lists of ideas and cross them off as they are executed. Get the whole place action-minded.

Top and bottom of the company usually love it. Middle management feels threatened. "If people are going to be setting their own standards and designing their own jobs in work teams, what do they need me for?" One answer is to give each foreman the authority to try any idea costing under $150 on the spot without further approval. Most of them have never had that before.

You can design and install a Scanlon plan yourself, but if you must have a consultant, the best are: Fred Lesieur of Novato, California, and Carl Frost of Lansing, Michigan.

TWO SCANLON STORIES

Lincoln Electric in Cleveland, Ohio, makes arc-welding equipment. In 1934 they were going belly up. The owner put in a Scanlon plan. Since then the cost of steel, copper, labor, and everything else they use has gone up six- or sevenfold. Last I heard, Lincoln was still selling their arc welders at the *1934 price*. In 1982, workers were paid competitive base salaries and took home additional annual bonuses averaging over $30,000 each.

Scripture Press in Wheaton, Illinois, had two meetings (as above) with Donnelly and then installed their own Scanlon plan. A year later they asked Donnelly to come in and take a reading. Donnelly found that the principal problem was the feeling of guilt workers had about the size of their bonuses for doing things they would have gladly done for nothing if they had been asked. Last I heard, the plan was going strong too.

If you have a plant manager and a labor leader with good will and common sense, you won't believe how spectacular the results will be.

SECRECY: A CHILD'S GARDEN OF DISEASES

Secrecy is totally bad. It defeats the crusade for justice, which doesn't flourish in the dark.

Did you ever ask yourself why there's a private payroll? Or why all wages and salaries aren't posted on the bulletin board? According to the lore of the free-enterprise system, money is really a scorecard. So why aren't the scores posted?*

Of course, the company would have a revulsion (or a revolution) if everybody had to look squarely at a list showing the salaries of the president and his nephew, who are paid four times what they're worth, and the salaries of Izzy, Derek, and Susie, who are making a third of what they're worth.

In the case of most marketing or new product planning, secrecy is sinister. It defeats your loyal opposition and protects you from your best friends when you need them most. Secrecy implies either:

1. *What I'm doing is so horrible I don't dare tell you.*
   or
2. *I don't trust you (anymore).*

---

*I'm not suggesting that you should post salaries. For one thing, it would overemphasize the importance of money. But you shouldn't tolerate a situation in which you're *ashamed* to post them. Like you are.

SECRETARY, FREEDOM FROM A

For years I had the standard executive equipment—a secretary. Most of them very good. Then I used the Man from Mars approach. Then I didn't have a secretary. Here's my analysis:

Before   *After*

TELEPHONE

Jane took all my calls and made all my calls (it really has to be all one or all the other). Two of the many games we played: "How long shall I let it ring before I decide she's not there?" "Shall I interrupt his meeting with this call?" (How many meetings, finally at the nitty-gritty, are interrupted by your secretary asking if you want to take a call, and you never seem to

The telephone operators took all my calls until eleven in the morning, saying, "May I have Mr. Townsend call you back?" Then at eleven, they'd send all the call messages in, start putting incoming calls through, and I would do the dialing myself. Result: Nobody mad. (Note, no offense because when she offers to have me call back, she hasn't asked

Before

get back on the track
whether you take the call
or not?)

After

who you are.) My calls
were concentrated in a
forty-five-minute period.
I'm on the phone first
(one up). Same thing from
lunch until four o'clock,
when the afternoon call
messages were sent in,
and incoming calls were
put through again.

APPOINTMENTS

I'd come back from a
one-day trip or even a
long lunch to find my calendar cluttered with ap-
pointments with my own
people.

Since there was no one to
make an appointment
with, people would stick
their heads in. If I wasn't
there, they'd come back
later, or change their
minds. Interruptions? A
few. But that's what I'm
there for.

Before	After
MAIL	
Jane would read it first. What with interruptions, it was generally the next morning before I got the replies back for signature.	Had two sets of note pads. One with just my name. The other, for strangers who wrote to the office, had my name, title, address, phone number. Handwritten replies.
	Advantages: Impressed the recipients. No files. Can be done on trips, weekends, early morning, evening. Lots faster. The infrequent letter that needed typing was done by staff services. If I wanted a Xerox of my note, I'd write "copy" in the corner.
FILES	
Jane filed copies of everything. Just to be sure.	Emptied all three file cabinets. What I kept

Before

Spent a lot of time at the Xerox machine or in transit. Finally had to have more space for her third four-drawer file cabinet.

After

filled half the file drawer in my desk. When that filled up, I'd weed it back to half. If you ever get a serious antitrust action, the thing that will hang you (even if you're innocent) will be Jane's files.

TRIPS

One of my close associates had a great secretary. Whenever he called in from out of town to get or leave messages, she was "away from her desk." And when he came back, she would have all the mail and memos and appointments spread out so he couldn't find his desk for two days.

When I called in, the telephone operators had my messages. The mailroom also had a rubber stamp: "I'm away. Please handle this in your own style and don't tell me what you did. Thanks. R.C.T." They'd open the mail, stamp it, route it appropriately. When I got back—clean desk.

Morning coffee, in-box, out-box, Xeroxing, and other matters were handled by staff services. An important thing I learned was that my secretary had been acting like an assistant-to. Helping me where I didn't want to be and couldn't be helped. Playing favorites with my associates. I got much closer to the people who reported to me when I didn't have a buffer state outside my office.

Working without a secretary depends on a good staff-services operation (*see* Staff Services [Steno Pool]). And making friends with the telephone operators, which is a breeze when they find out you're going to can your secretary. Telephone operators and executive secretaries are natural enemies.

Build a good staff-services setup and then try to persuade your executives to give it a good fair try for a month whenever secretaries quit, or get sick or go on vacation. In my case, unloading a secretary worked out like finding an extra four hours a day.

SMALL BUSINESS, STARTING A

Are you really ready for it?

It means 120-hour weeks instead of the 30-hour week (two-hour lunches) you're giving General Electric. Maybe you should spend some time getting in shape; start by eating right, exercising, and giving up smoking and drinking.

Is your spouse ready to be married to a worn-out stranger for five years?

Have you made your cash forecast? You think it's pretty conservative? You've allowed for Murphy's Law? Right. Now add six months on the front end before your first dollar of revenue comes in. Deduct 20 percent from your revenue estimates and add 20 percent to your expense estimates. If you're lucky, you may make this.

This new cash forecast means you'll have to raise several times as much money as you thought, which brings us to investors. Have as few as you can. If you have to go up to a couple of dozen in a Subchapter S corporation, for example, have them elect a spokesman who will be your only point of contact with the investors. Persuade them that your chances (and theirs) of success are greatly increased if you hold an all-day "Howedoin?" meeting with your spokesman (or with the whole group) once a quarter, not more frequently. It takes three precious days away from your business for one of these meetings: one to get ready, one to do it, and one to get over it.

Try to find a young able lawyer and a young able accountant who like your business idea and will give you services in return for stock. Hire employees one at a time and only when you're desperate. Assign them something to do that you've proven you can do, not something that you don't know how to do. You have to learn everything first (except accounting and law).

Use phantom shares when paying people with stock. And make sure you can and do recapture the shares when people leave the company for any reason. Pay them book value or appraised value but get the shares back. You don't want shareholders working for competitors or generally being a nuisance.

Stay as small as you can. Work out of your home as long as you can. Then your garage. Avoid any expensive ornaments like offices, furniture, or cars designed to impress the public or your friends. The only things you want to be impressive are your product or service, your financial statements, and the smiles on the faces of your customers.

SMALL COMPANIES

. . . trying to make the transition to big publicly owned companies tend to make the same mistake.

They look at General Motors and see finance committees, executive committees, planning departments, advertising departments, marketing departments, personnel departments, management development departments, and public relations departments, and they say, "Aha, so that's how they do it!" And a year later they're out of business. If Alfred Sloan had started with all that crap, there wouldn't be a General Motors to look at.

If you're a small or medium-size business trying to make the grade, you're going to have to take on a few of the burdens of the publicly owned companies. But only a few. And for that reason carefully examine every new expense and activity to see whether it's a necessity or an ornament.

If *your* problem is to keep your share of the market below 55 percent and your operating profit margin below 20 percent, then you're an oligopolist and can afford to act like one. But I'm afraid you'll be like the poor old lady who thought all she had to do to become an opera singer was to drink lots of heavy cream—you'll be confusing fat with muscle.

STAFF SERVICES (STENO POOL)*

You can't call it "steno pool." It brings to mind the dregs of the office. My steno pool I call "staff services." And there must be a better name. It serves the brightest executives, including the chief executive officer, because they don't have secretaries.

The staff-services office is luxuriously furnished and its people are recruited from the ranks of the best secretaries in the area. And paid top salaries.

One of them brings you your coffee, empties your outbasket, does your Xeroxing, brings your mail, poses as your secretary (to a telephone caller who won't believe you don't have a secretary), takes dictation in your office or from your Dictaphone belts.

Since there are, say, ten of them for twenty executives, your secretary is never sick. Since these people are paid as much as the secretaries of executives who insist on having their own, and since the day goes faster if you're busy (and what secretary for one man is constantly busy?), their morale is high and the pressure is from secretaries trying to get *into* the group, not out of it.

Please get it through your head: You're not trying to

See also Telephone Operators.

save money. That was the steno-pool idea. You're trying to improve the secretarial services without spending any more money and without having a lot of half-occupied people trying to look busy so they won't be asked to help someone who's not their boss.

START-UP:
CLEAN THE BLACKBOARD

If you ever get a chance to start a manufacturing operation, strike a blow against the division between labor
and management when you do it:

Put everybody on salary, including the janitor.

Everybody gets the same benefits package.

No reserved parking—first come, first served. This
benefits the officers—it's harder to tell when they're
goofing off if they don't have an assigned parking
space.

Executives responsible for a mill or plant have their offices and secretaries *in* that mill or plant, not in the
executive office building.

A paneled board room with overstuffed chairs suitable
for directors' tender butts will be located *in* each mill
and plant. Think about it: the decisions made in those
board rooms are a hell of a lot more profitable than
most of the ones made in the corporate board room.

Comfortable, air-conditioned, soundproofed rest and
eating areas in each plant and mill.

Put the workers' lockers and the janitor's office in the

executive office building. It's a more important symbol of what you think of them than calling them "associates" as Honda does. Besides, if you want to spread some bit of information around the company, all you have to do is walk down the hall and tell the janitor.

Free coffee for everybody, dummy, not just the executives and their secretaries.

Suggestion: The big labor unions, made strong by stupid managements of the past, are in a weak position. Let us not be stupid again! Close the gaps wherever you can between executives and white-collar and blue-collar workers. America's productivity depends on it.

STOCKHOLDERS

As is well known, the big corporation's priorities are:

1. *Care and feeding of the chief executive, his entourage, and the board of directors (mostly his friends, put there by him to ensure the tranquillity of his reign)*
2. *Management*
3. *Employees*
4. *Customers*
5. *(Way down the line) Stockholders*

Only very rarely is the stockholder mentioned in a company. I suggest a different set of priorities:

1. *Stockholders. Turn the management and as many employees as possible into stockholders—and with enough stock so they think of themselves as owners.**
2. *This makes the customer important.*
3. *Management and employees are taken care of by their succcess as stockholders as well as by a healthier company that can afford to pay top salaries.*
4. *In my utopian corporation, directors are last priority. They are paid nothing, attend meetings because they are stockholders, get monthly figures, meet quarterly*

---

*Professional managers are cautious because they have to prove they're right; owner-managed companies take more chances and their timing is better because it's their money on the line and they have the right to try something they can't prove.

for an all-day report on the state and trend of the business, and are concerned solely with putting out dividends and chief executives.

SUGGESTION BOXES: MAKE THEM INTO BIRDHOUSES

The way to get good ideas for increasing productivity and profits is:

1. *Install profit sharing* (see *Incentive Compensation and Profit Sharing*). *If you're in a mature, non-growth company, consider a Scanlon-type plan for cost reduction* (see *Scanlon Plan*).
2. *Train your foremen to meet with their workers in idea sessions. Give foremen the authority to try ideas costing up to $150 each without further approval.*

These sessions are efficient because poor ideas are shot down immediately by peers; good ideas get immediate support and stand a good chance if tried right away.

The wrong way: having workers tell an agent or delegate who in turn garbles the idea in a meeting with other delegates.

An even worse way: suggestion boxes. Lots of people with good ideas can't put them down on paper, and are afraid of looking stupid.

3. *Feedback. Help figure out monthly or, better yet,*

*weekly reports showing costs, productivity—whatever.
Keep showing the results even if they turn sour. Don't
protect people from the truth.*

Now get cracking on those birdhouses.

T TAX ADVICE

You ask your law firm to recommend a tax specialist from among their partners, and you ask your public accounting firm to do the same. You talk to the two of them and try to get them interested in your business. Then, as in the choice of a lawyer, you pick the one who will give you his home phone and who will listen to your problem, ask questions, and then call you back within twenty-four hours with his opinion.

Big-company-style tax specialists are murder. They judge themselves by how many pros and cons they can dream up, and how many alternate methods might be "worth investigating." You need somebody who will say, "If I were you and had to make a decision and then get back to minding the store, I'd do this."

TEAMS, TWO-MAN— GOOD AND BAD

I've long held the opinion that a two-man chief executive is the answer. Even Reagan, who is doing less than any President since Eisenhower, has a schedule most of us couldn't survive for long. It's no wonder to me that our country has been in a leadership crisis for most of this century.

But two-man teams aren't easy.

The two men have to complement each other, and above all trust each other implicitly. They both have to have a sense of humor and they have to enjoy working together. Each must respect the other's fundamental instincts, not just in talk but in action. If you're about to do something that your partner might be nervous about, you ask if he has a conviction against it. The "do you have a conviction?" game is about the only way to keep from driving each other up the wall.

The worst two-man team I ever saw tried to act like the Bobbsey twins even though 3,000 miles normally separated them. They tried to keep each other totally informed at all times *in advance*. I suppose the idea was that then they'd share the responsibility for mistakes. But in addition to being time-consuming, this method *reduces* accountability. "Oh well, Bill knew about it in advance and went along with the idea." Instead of "Holy mackerel, I'm out here all by myself, I better find a way to make this work, or kill it before it gets out of control."

The best two-man team I ever saw started with the philosophy: Neither of us is very good, but our weaknesses (and strengths) may be compensating. Like yang and yin, man and wife. We expect to make a lot of mistakes, but we hope to have the courage to correct them no matter how silly we look in the process. If we do our best, split up the chores, check in advance on strategic matters, and keep each other informed after the fact on the daily disasters, we'll have fun.

Sample telephone conversations:

1. *"If you don't have a conviction, I'm going to do this about that . . ."*
2. *"Unless you object, I'm going to take on this [task, opportunity, problem, obstacle]. I'll let you know how I did."* That means I'll call you in a week or six months or whenever it's over. It doesn't mean I'll keep you posted on each day's triumph or tribulation.
3. *"This needs doing. Will you do it? I'm no good at it."*
4. *"Do you know about . . .?" "Yes, I'm going to take*

care of it when the time is right." Or "*Good grief, I forgot all about it. I'll do it right now. Thanks.*"

5. "*You remember I told you I'd take care of . . . Well, this is what I finally did. This is what I should have done. This is what it cost the company. How's that for wasting money?*"

6. In the matter of strategic (expensive-to-correct) decisions: "*I've thought through the XYZ matter. There are three ways to go: the first looks like this; the second looks like this; and the third looks like this. I've got no real conviction but I'm inclined to* [or *I feel strongly that we should*] *go the second route.*"

In this instance and at this point it is strongly advisable for the speaker to sit back and listen. Often he'll hear: "*It's a tough choice, do whatever you think is right,*" or "*Sounds right to me.*" Occasionally, a good listener will hear: "*You fathead! What's the matter with the fourth way?*" I've saved a lot of money listening for that sound, no matter how I cringed at the time.

I've known three-man chief executive teams that worked where two were in one location and one in another. But not very well and not for long.

TELEPHONE OPERATORS

If I ever design a head office, executive row will look like the cubicles of a Trappist monastery, and the telephone-switchboard area will look like a Turkish harem. Money spent on offices for the management is largely wasted. If they are any good, it will be apparent to anyone after a few minutes no matter how plain or fancy their office is.

On the other hand, how would you like to try doing the telephone operator's job for a day? Remember, you're the company's first contact with the outside world— you've got to be alert and bright and helpful and quick. You've got to know where everybody is all the time. I'd spend money to make the switchboard people comfortable. The best operators in the area would be lined up for the job.

THANKS

A really neglected form of compensation.

TIME:
THREE THOUGHTS ON IT

Small companies should be fun. The key people frequently work six days and all hours and get very expert. That's a 20 percent edge over the nine-to-five five-days-a-week big-business operation.

New people need time to earn their place on a team. New systems need time to shake down. Lots of people are quick with the torpedoes on new people and new systems. Give them time.

Some meetings should be long and leisurely. Some should be mercifully brief. A good way to handle the latter is to hold the meeting with everybody standing up. The meetees won't believe you at first. Then they get very uncomfortable and can hardly wait to get the meeting over with. If you have more than one comfortable chair for office visitors, move to a smaller office.

TIME TO FIRE THE CHIEF EXECUTIVE OFFICER?— A TEST FOR THE BOARD OF DIRECTORS

When a company starts going sour, and the CEO no longer has what it takes to turn it around, he starts hating to come to work and he begins to get his satisfaction out of ego trips.

If your CEO is enjoying more than three of these cruises, you'd better put a twenty-four-hour watch on him. If he scores above four, he seriously needs firing:

1. *He becomes president of the trade association.*
2. *He becomes chairman of the hospital fund drive.*
3. *He goes on (another) board of directors.*
4. *He accepts (another) foreign decoration.*
5. *He takes the company plane to Aspen or Palm Springs or Europe with his family or girlfriend.*
6. *He forms a committee of the board to consider the creation of golden parachutes.*
7. *He decides he needs more than two secretaries (executive assistants, or whatever he calls them).*
8. *The gap between his total compensation and the next layer's is getting wider, not narrower, as he approaches retirement.*

9. *He starts appearing on TV and in magazines in the company ads.*

Important: Notwithstanding any of the above, if the old boy starts saying things like "We've got a lot of good young people coming along, but the senior management is a little weak," or if he hires a search firm to look for a potential successor, he should be put out to pasture immediately.

TITLES ARE HANDY TOOLS*

There is a trade-off here. In one way, titles are a form of psychic compensation, and if too many titles are distributed, the currency is depreciated. But a title is also a tool. If our salesman is a vice-president and yours is a sales rep, and both are in a waiting room, guess who gets in first and gets the most attention.

If you find you can't get applicants for menial jobs, maybe your titles are obsolete. Nobody today can admit to his woman that he's a clerk or a busboy. One airline improved a bad situation by changing "ramp service clerk" to "ramp service engineer." A restaurant cured a chronic busboy shortage by changing the title to "logistics engineer."

*For further thoughts on titles, *see* Chairman of the Executive Committee.

TOO MUCH VS. TOO LITTLE

Too little is almost always better than too much.

Space: Too much brings out the worst in empire builders. They'll fill up the excess so fast you'll wind up with too little again. Too little makes you creative in your use of people. Too much puts the company emphasis on office grandeur, not on service and performance.*

People: One person with only half a job can wander around and do real damage in his or her spare time. The best organizations are sufficiently understaffed so that if somebody does something that overlaps or invades your area of responsibility, your second reaction is: "Great! If you've got time to do that, *you* do it from now on." This feeling comes right after the first flash of territorial hostility. Organizations that have time to get into jurisdictional disputes are almost always overstaffed.

Money: A tight budget brings out the best creative instincts in man. Give him unlimited funds and he won't come up with the best way to a result. Man is a complicating animal. He only simplifies under pressure. Put him under some financial pressure. He'll scream in

---

*At Avis I resisted demands for more space at headquarters. While we grew from $30 million to $75 million, we stayed in 30,000 square feet. "Double-decker desks" was a common joke. When the demands became too insistent, I let a couple of units move into neighboring buildings. But only units with a profit center of their own. At least there you have the performance yardstick of profit. But let a service function like accounting move out, and if separation doesn't work, they may take out their frustration in empire building before you realize what's happening.

anguish. Then he'll come up with a plan which, to his own private amazement, is not only less expensive but also faster and better than his original proposal, which you sent back.

TRAINING

The only way I know to get somebody trained is on the job.

The first time I learned this was by accident. I'd laboriously recruited an assistant (note: not an assistant-to). By the time I'd offered the job and he'd accepted I was pretty sure I had a good man. But the earliest he could come to work was the day I left for vacation. Turmoil! Should I go? For the wrong reasons I went.

Thrown in the deep end, he learned some plain and fancy swimming while I was away. And he developed some valuable relationships in those three weeks that might never have developed if I'd been there. He got in the habit of growing and has never stopped.

If you have more than one possible successor, *never* anoint a favorite. You'll stop the healthy competition for your job and paint a bull's-eye on your heir's shirtfront. I did it once, and the organization tore him to shreds. Better to keep an open-minded show-me attitude toward all contenders.

Every time I left the office for more than a week, I'd write the following memo:

To:	*People who report to me*
Date:	*Today*
cc:	*Mailroom*
	Owner
	Telephone operators

I've gone away. Until I get back Henry is chief executive officer. Please don't hold up decisions. Anything you do in my absence will have my complete support when I return. R.C.T.

Two things about this. Rotate the acting successor if you can. Otherwise you've named your heir. And don't say where you've gone or when you'll be back.

Remember, you really want them to make some important decisions and some mistakes (*see* Mistakes). That's how they grow.

TURNAROUND

If you get picked to head up and turn an old mossback division or department around, here's what you do.

Call in everybody who reports to you one at a time. Ask them what they do, how the outfit works, what makes it tick, and eventually what goes wrong and what's missing. Mainly you listen.

Then you go out and listen to the people who report to them. Soon you're out on the shop floor or in the field or with the customers—listening. No decisions. No promises. Just listen and remember.

Now go back and talk to your lieutenants and listen to their reactions to what you've learned. Then back to the front lines again.

After a couple of months you'll know:

1. *Who the few unsung heroes and heroines are up and down the line.*
2. *Who the sons of bitches are.*
3. *What rules, regulations, practices, and policies should be stopped right now.*

Get your lieutenants together and hammer out some decisions to fire or retire the sons of bitches, reward the

heroes and heroines, and cancel the rules and regulations. Lock the door until you're all in agreement on
some program. The changes shouldn't leak out over the
days as you write memos to each other.

When you're in agreement, here's how you execute it:

1. *Each hero gets his reward from his boss, not from
   you.*
2. *Each son of a bitch gets fired or retired by his boss.
   His boss can blame you and then you get to listen to
   the son of a bitch.*
3. *No brave-new-world speech from* anybody. *The announcement about the rules and regulations comes in
   the regular way.*

Now you've begun. You've got the division's attention.
From here on it's a matter of how many ideas you and
your troops can surface, identify, and try.

Momentum is important. To keep the ideas coming you
have to spend at least a week a month out in the field
or on the shop floor or with customers. Pretty soon
some of your lieutenants will start doing that too and
then the division is on its way.

Another example. Three divisions report to you. One is
not making it. Each year they reorganize (or pretend to)
and fail again. You've run out of time and you want to
minimize the risk of failing again.

Here's what you do. Fire or retire the division leader. Take his job yourself. *Move to his office. Repeat: move to his office.* Call in the people who reported to him. Tell them you're their new boss and then proceed as above, working full time for that one division.

Several things will happen.

First, you'll be astounded at how well your other two divisions do without you.

Second, you'll be amazed at the energy and excitement you generate in the sick division by getting closer to the problem.

Third, within six months you'll have identified and promoted from within the right person to lead the division out of the wilderness (*see* Hiring *and* Promotion, from Within), and you'll be back in your old office feeling much better.

Don't forget to give some appropriate rewards to the two divisions who did so well without you.

U UNDERPAID

Some good people become badly underpaid. If you're in this spot, but like your work, cheer up; all is not lost.

Resign. Go to the personnel department. Fill in the forms. Apply for your old position. Under "salary objective," put down what you should be paid.

If your diagnosis is correct, you'll be far and away the best-qualified applicant for your old job and cheap at the new price. When I bullied a griping friend into doing this, he ended up with a 30 percent pay raise, in a company that didn't believe in paying people.

If they don't rehire you because of "regulations," it's time you left the company anyway, because they've got the tail on the front of the dog.

V VACATION POLICY: GO WHEN YOU PLEASE

Just like office hours, vacations for people who make more than $25,000 should be left up to each individual. No responsible person will abuse the freedom. Your worst job will be running your best people out of town when they need some play time.

# WASHINGTON, D.C., RELATIONS WITH

Businessmen often underestimate the number of able, conscientious, and zealous people working for government in Washington—and Albany, Springfield, and Sacramento. They're usually overworked and underpaid. And motivated primarily by pride and faith in what they're doing. Try treating them that way.

Don't use a prestigious Washington law firm to represent you in ordinary* government relations. All the ready-made defenses click into place when Tommy Boggs's boys call up.

But when your lawyer from Terre Haute telephones, it's an event. It's different. They have no idea who he is, and no way of making sure. He can walk in and say, "You're my government . . . help me." And they will. And love him for asking. It's a refreshing change for them from the hotshot New York and Washington lawyers who have all the answers and are telling . . . not asking.

---

*In a major emergency, however, there is no substitute for Joe Califano or someone of that ilk.

WEARING OUT
YOUR WELCOME

Nobody should be chief executive officer of anything for more than five or six years. By then he's stale, bored, and utterly dependent on his own clichés—though they may have been revolutionary ideas when he first brought them to the office.

Also, decisions aren't based on consensus, but on one man's view of what's best for the organization. And that means even the best decisions make some people unhappy. After five or six years a good chief will have absorbed all the hostility he can take, and his decisions will be reflecting a desire to avoid pain rather than to do what's right.

In 1940, when Sewell Avery had completed eight years as chief executive of Montgomery Ward, that company's common stock was valued in the stock market at $200 million, compared to $500 million for competitor Sears, Roebuck. Avery stayed fourteen more years and a race became no contest. In mid-1967, before Montgomery Ward disappeared from the stock market by merger, its common stock was valued at $400 million—a double in twenty-seven years. Sears, Roebuck in mid-1967 was worth $9 billion—eighteen times as much as in 1940.

Lesson for stockholders and directors: If the chief executive doesn't retire gracefully after five or six years—throw the rascal out.

WHY BIG-COMPANY CEOs AREN'T LEADERS*

Because they stopped taking chances when they got in line for the top job.

And because the rewards of the top job make it impossible to lead.

Let's say you've just become the Big Guy. You arrive at work in a limo, you climb out of the car in the company garage and get into your private elevator, which takes you to your suite of offices. Your three secretaries are waiting to protect you from any unpleasantness. In your private dining room for lunch, you meet with satisfied customers and senior officers only. Anything controversial has to be written up, predigested, and sugarcoated before it gets to you. Your calendar is loaded with outside board and committee meetings and social engagements with your powerful new friends outside the company. After a few months of this, you've lost touch with all the colleagues who helped you get the top job, and you have no idea what's going on.

Of course, it's a nice way to spend your last five years. But you're not leading.

How about the next layer of management?

*Mr. Iacocca seems to be the exception that proves the rule, but the jury's still out.

They've all reached the golden escalator where noses are clean, voices subdued, records unbesmirched by mistakes, and the key word is WAIT.

In fact, there is no leadership. The top corporate staff are presiding over the remaining momentum through their mastery of the techniques of meeting and report writing—all in the service of not rocking the boat.

Remember the young Turk who made his way up the organization through his successful risk taking?

When he got to the golden escalator he started playing it safe.

Ferchrissake, the whole top of the pyramid is busy playing it safe, and there's no surer way to bankrupt the business!

The solution? When *you* become CEO, give up all those perks and distractions and take your top team out on the road for five years looking for ideas, problems, and opportunities, and teaching the organization to take chances again.

When you retire—*that's* when you take the chauffeur, the limo, the private elevator, the suite of offices, the secretaries, and the outside directorships.

Just make sure you don't bother the new CEO. He'll be too busy to talk to you.

WORKERS SHOULD OWN COMPANY STOCK

American free-enterprise system! Bullshit!

What we've got now is the management free-enterprise system. The people aren't involved in it. Ninety-five percent of your people have never even seen a stock certificate.

But don't *give* them stock; give them the chance to buy it. The percentage signing up to buy will tell you what they think of the company.

And don't worry if your board of directors doesn't approve of union members buying stock. Their thinking is part of the problem.

"Since I got my first stock certificate, I haven't been throwing away pencils," said Linda _____ of the Dana Corporation.*

Think what that attitude will do. Think of a machine operator on a broach bar. He can do beautiful work, or he can break the tool and cost you $5,000. Think of a salesman on a call. Think of a punch-press operator working on a compound die. That could cost you ten big ones.

---

*Dana's stock-purchase plan evolved like this: Minimum purchase of $2 per pay period—a maximum of 10 percent of the W-2. After four years, 29 percent had signed up. Then they added a company contribution tied to Dana's pre-tax profit margin: at 5 percent the company would add 30 percent to each purchase; at 5½ percent, 35 percent; and so forth. Ten years later, 80 percent of the people were shareholders. "If somebody was doing something wrong, one of his buddies would say, 'Hey, you're hurtin' all of us.' Now that's management of the people, by the people, for the people—people management," says Ren McPherson, former Dana CEO.

CEO.

Get with it, Mac! If 70 percent of your people think of themselves as shareholders, it's worth at least two percentage points on your company's pre-tax profit margin.

With 2 percent you can beat anybody in the country. Or Japan.

APPENDIX: RATE YOUR BOSS AS A LEADER

Score each characteristic from 0 to 10

He is

1. . . . *available. If I have a problem I can't solve, he is there. But he is forceful in making me do my level best to bring in solutions, not problems.* _____

2. . . . *inclusive. Quick to let me in on information or people who might be useful to me or stimulating or of long-term professional interest.* _____

3. . . . *humorous. Has a full measure of the Comic Spirit in his make-up. Laughs even harder when the joke's on him.* _____

4. . . . *fair. And concerned about me and how I'm doing. Gives credit where credit is due, but holds me to my promise.* _____

5. . . . *decisive. Determined to get at those little unimportant (how they are decided) decisions which can tie up organizations for days.* _____

6. . . . *humble. Admits his own mistakes openly—learns from them and expects his people to do the same.* _____

7. . . . *objective. Knows the apparently important (like a visiting director) from the truly important (a meeting of his own people) and goes where he is needed.* _____

8. . . . *tough. Won't let top management or important outsiders waste his time or his people's time. Is more jealous of his people's time than he is of his own.* _____

9. . . . *effective. Teaches me to bring him my mistakes with what I've learned (if anything) and done about them (if anything). Teaches me not to interrupt him with possible good news on which no action is needed.* _____

10. . . . *patient. Knows when to bite the
bullet until I solve my own problem.*_____

*Total**_____

**This is your boss's rating as a leader on a scale of 0 to 100. If it's below 50, look
for another job.*

ACKNOWLEDGMENTS

Having no secretary and an unreadable hand, I was doubly blessed with the unfailing help of Starr Johnson (Moonlight West) and Angie Abbatello (Moonlight East). Thank you.

David Dushkin steered me to Bob Gottlieb and Tony Schulte at Knopf, for which I'm grateful: when you have to deal with a stark raving mad industry like book publishing, it's well to deal directly with the head lunatics. Emmet Hughes gave valuable thinking and criticism, for which I am grateful.

It would be unthinkable not to mention the educational value of my fourteen years at American Express. During those years (1948–62) the company was rich enough to do—and did—almost everything wrong. In that near-perfect learning environment I formed the valuable habit of observing what action was taken, considering the *opposite* course, and then working back, when necessary, to what really made sense.

For the past ten years, Donald Petrie and Jerry Hardy, two voices laughing hysterically in the institutional wilderness, have kept telling me that just because we were alone didn't mean that we were wrong. Without their ideas and reinforcement, I'd have probably given up before the conclusive (to us) opportunity to test this pattern of management came along.

March 1970